YOU CAN DRAW PORTRAITS

Colorized Edition

Technical Drawing
Mastering an Exact Likeness

YOU CAN DRAW PORTRAITS
Colorized Edition

Technical Drawing
Mastering an Exact Likeness

DAVID RITE

YOU CAN DRAW PORTRAITS
Colorized Edition
Technical Drawing
Mastering an Exact Likeness

For more information and a free tutorial you can visit David Rite's internet site at:

http://www.davidrite.com

Cover design/Photo Art by: **Steve Lee**

By using this publication, you agree and understand that it is for your personal and non-commercial use only and that it is not to be shared in any form whole or in part with another party. You agree to abide by the copyright laws of the United States and International Statutes as set forth to protect the rights of the copyright holder.

No part of this publication may be reproduced, stored in a retrieval system, or transmitted in any form or by any means, electronic, mechanical, photocopying, recording, scanning, or otherwise, without either the prior written permission of the Publisher or Author. Requests for permission should be addressed to www.davidrite.com. If any information contained herein is closely related to others work or text found in whole or in part, it is purely coincidental. All rights reserved under the Intellectual Copyright statutes and the International and Pan-American Copyright Conventions.

The information contained in this book is provided *'as is'* and without warranty of any kind. While the publisher and the author have used their best efforts in preparing and writing this book, they make no representations or warranties with respect to the accuracy or completeness of the contents of this book and specifically disclaim any implied warranties of merchantability or fitness for any purpose. No warranty may be created or extended by sales representatives or written sales materials. The advice and strategies contained herein may vary from person to person and situation. You should consult with professionals where appropriate.

Several classes and documents were collected from the author/contributors and the material is not entirely from one *"sitting"* or *"drawing session"*. Some illustrations may vary. The purchaser and/or reader*(s)* take upon themselves the entire responsibility as to the results and the performance of the information contained herein. In no event shall the Publisher, David Rite, or any Contributor to his work be liable for any loss of profit or any other commercial damages, including but not limited to special, incidental, consequential, or other damages including any injuries that may be suffered while using the information and materials suggested in the David Rite books.

Published in United States.
This book publication Cataloging-in-Publication-Data
David Rite, 2021 ©
ISBN: 978-1-7358868-2-4

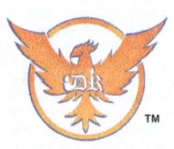

"The three great essentials to achieve anything worth while are, first, hard work; second, stick-to-itiveness; third, common sense."

~ Thomas A. Edison

Special Thanks To:

My Loving Family
For all of their support and patience during the creation of the 'You Can' Book Series.

~

My Dear Friends
Who have inspired and gone the twain with me during my career as an artist.
You know who you are!

~

Divine Essential Healing
Your contributions towards furthering my artistic career has effected the sum of my life.

Affectionately,

~ David Rite

At the request

of many patrons, teachers, and students
I have taken the time to make this
special colorized edition.

~

You Can Draw Portraits

is now accented in color.
This experience in color will add a little flare into
an otherwise black and white drawing book.
It is visually stimulating!

~

Thanks

for all the requests to have,
"You Can Draw Portraits
Technical Drawing Mastering an Exact Likeness"
in color!

**We hope you enjoy this newly colorized edition
of You Can Draw Portraits!**

PREFACE

For years I have seen the need for an art book that was well organized, easy to understand, and principle based, which would enable anyone to draw portraits with an exact likeness. This book was written to fill that need. I have laid out the principles of drawing in a step by step method that will direct and assist anyone to take control of their drawings. When these techniques are applied the results will be the same every time; *Perfect, Exact, and Beautiful!*

I cannot overstate the importance of an accurate drawing especially when we are contemplating making a portrait. This book will be an aid in furthering your ability to draw with conviction, confidence, and accuracy that many artists only dream of. By utilizing my 'You Can' books, you can make your artistic dreams come true.

To demonstrate the drawing techniques that the classical artists used in creating their masterpieces; I have chosen from William Bouguereau's collection of works, the beautiful oil painting the girl with *'Daisies'*. This famous traditionalist is one of my favorite painters whose realistic classical paintings are ideal for instructing the method for drawing. I will concentrate on the foundation of the portrait, the drawing, and mainly focus on the face and hair to show the process of draftsmanship necessary in obtaining an exact likeness.

The analogy I often use while teaching my students about the importance of a drawing in reference to portrait drawing and painting is this; the drawing can be compared to a beautifully adorned cake. *"The drawing"* is like the fundamental aspect or base of the desert, the *"cake"*, while its ornamental frosting is representational of the portrait's painting or *"color"*. The actual substance, the drawing, is all in the cake while its attraction is in its color or frosting. It takes time to develop the talent to enable one to masterfully create a delicious cake. It takes even more time to obtain the polishing skills used in decorating its' intricate details or the icing. In this book, I will take you through the creating process of drawing a portrait and give you the necessary tools to complete a portrait successfully.

This book can serve as the foundation of your art book collection. It will increase your knowledge while you are developing the talents required to complete a portrait with an exact likeness. Thomas Edison once stated, *"To my mind the old masters are not art; their value is in their scarcity"*. We are in a new age where there is no need for scarcity. I will use the old masters' techniques for drawing to demonstrate how you can become a master of portrait drawing today. I recommend that you also get my *'You can Paint Portraits'* book to add to your art library. These two books used in conjunction will aid you in understanding the whole process for completing a portrait in oil.

I acknowledge with gratitude the encouragement, inspiration, and influential help of many individuals. I wanted to make special mention of them, yet there are too many to list here. Nevertheless, they have given me stability in my writing and validity in my art.

If you have a passion for the Fine Arts, share it! Recommend these *'You Can'* books to everyone!

They will take you from where you are to where you want to be!

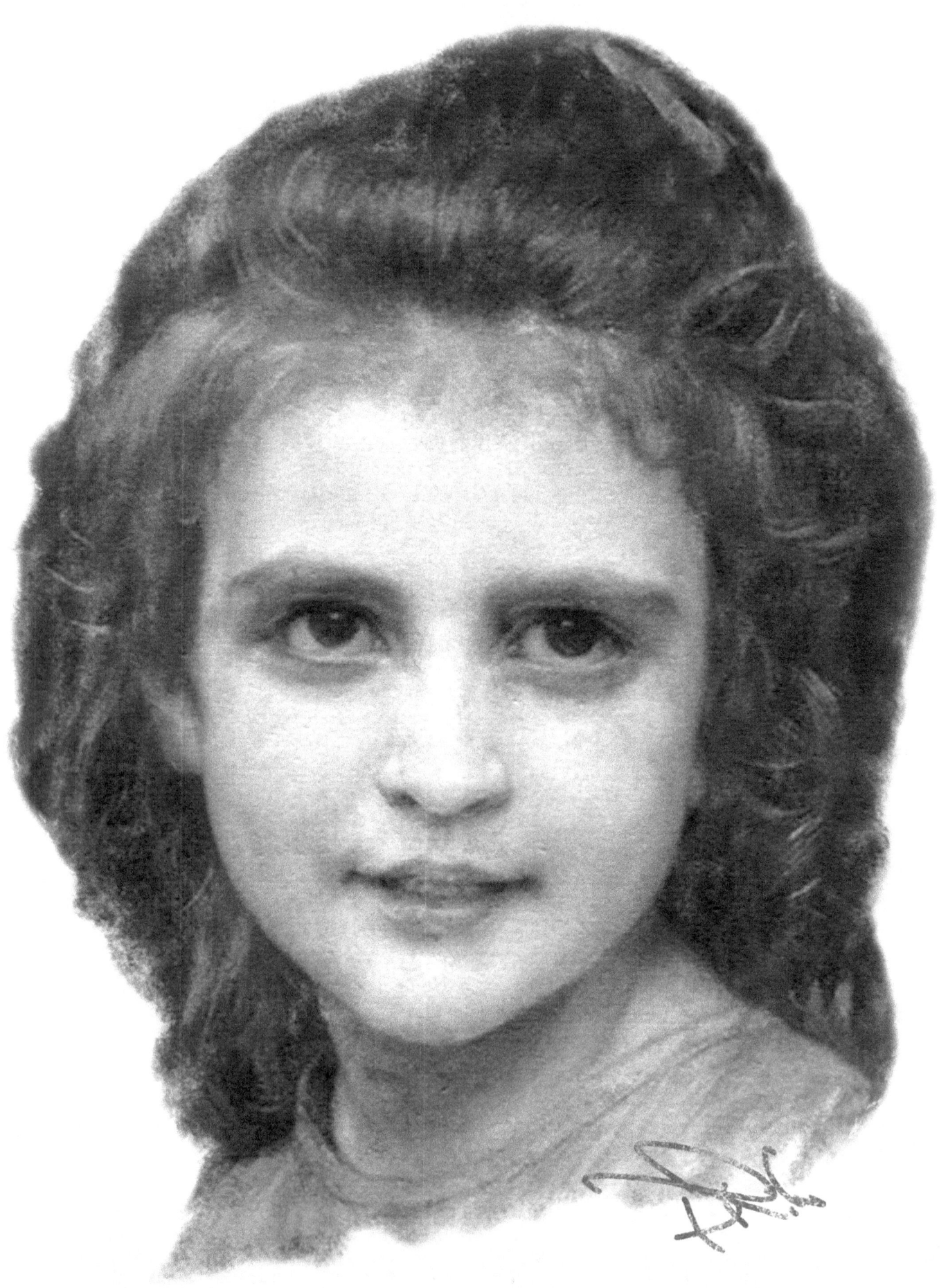

CONTENTS

SECTION 1 — INTRODUCTION — 5
- Welcome Information
- Materials Needed
- Three-Step Process
- The 12-Step Formula

SECTION 2 — DRAWING WITH CONFIDENCE — 15
- Introduction to Drawing
- Things to Remember
- Lights and Shadows
- Perspective/Composition/Tones
- The Standard Proportions

SECTION 3 — DRAWING I — 25
- Lets Get Started
- Finding the Map Points for the Width of the Face

SECTION 4 — DRAWING II — 41
- Drawing the Eyes
- Completion of the Eyes

SECTION 5 — DRAWING III — 53
- Finding Map Points for the Lips/Ear/Nose
- Drawing the Nose and Mouth
- Drawing the Nose *(detailed)*
- Drawing the Mouth *(detailed)*

SECTION 6 — DRAWING IV — 71
- Establishing and Completing Chin/Cheek Lines
- Beginning the Forehead Lines
- Smoothing the Face
- Beginning the Hair and Neck

CONTENTS

SECTION 7   **DRAWING V**   **85**
        Stages for drawing the portrait:
        Finishing the hair and neck

SECTION 8   **APPENDIX**   **117**
        Appendix

SECTION 9   **GLOSSARY**   **131**
        Glossary
        Materials Defined

INTRODUCTION:
Section: 1

"An investment in knowledge pays the best interest."

~ Benjamin Franklin

INTRODUCTION

I have created this book for the many talented and wonderful people who have expressed to me their enthusiasm to learn how to draw. These individuals have often declared that they would love to be able to pick up a pencil and draw what they see. I have found that in order to produce a beautiful drawing; it takes time, knowledge, and practice. This book contains the necessary techniques which will enable anyone to master the art of drawing. I would like to welcome everyone to the 'You Can Draw Portraits: Technical Drawing Mastering an Exact Likeness', which is the finest art training book for beginners, students, advanced artists, and teachers today.

To the artist in all of us: There is good news for all of those who would like to draw, but for some reason may not have the inward ability or confidence to do so. This book shows that there is a tried and proven instructional method that can lead anyone logically through the necessary steps to become a confident artist and draw what they see!

The craft of drawing is the ability of an artist to draw accurately what he or she sees. In the following pages I will show you the three proven techniques that I use and teach others. I want to encourage everyone to become a student of the three-step method of drawing. It is the key to success for increasing your drawing skills. This new endeavor will stimulate you intellectually and sharpen your artistic instincts. So, get ready to hone your skills. At the end of this material, you will have received the necessary tools to draw exactly what you see. Remember, that learning a new skill, which will bring your drawing ability into focus, will require practice and strict adherence to the three-step method. The key to drawing is repetition of the three-steps. So, my advice is to *practice, practice, practice, and draw, draw, draw!*

After mastering all these steps, I would encourage everyone to share their knowledge with others, by becoming a teacher of these successful techniques!

To all teachers: I have talked with art teachers that would like to teach drawing, yet they were not sure how to impart their knowledge to students, especially to those pupils that did not seem to have the innate intuitive ability to draw. This book is designed to aid anyone, that wishes to teach, by increasing their ability to instruct others through the classical drafting techniques taught by the masters. Therefore, I have included in each section detailed examples, which will enable anyone to inspire and motivate their students.

Your proficiency in drawing will improve as you teach your students these lessons. Everyone should have this book as the foundation of learning how to draw. By applying these techniques, you will experience new advances in your drawing career. Your teaching income potential will increase, I am sure, and that too will be a welcomed bonus.

NOW IT'S UP TO YOU!

You Can Draw Portraits:
Technical Drawing-Mastering an Exact Likeness *(Introduction)*

MATERIALS NEEDED:

The following suggested materials have distinct characteristics that can help in blending, smoothing, and softening your drawing. The right materials are crucial while working on a portrait drawing. It is so much easier to draw when you have the right tool for the right job. The materials listed below will help in attaining the essential, but subtle tonal values in a portrait.

See Section 9 *(Materials Defined)* for more information about each item listed below.

Materials needed in alphabetical order:

1. **CHARCOAL PAPER** *(FINE TEXTURED)*   (1)

2. **CHARCOAL STICK** *(FINE VINE)*

3. **CHARCOAL STICK** *(NUMBER 9)*   (2)

4. **CHARCOAL STUMPS**

5. **KNEADED ERASERS**

6. **MEASURING TOOL**

7. **TORILLONS**

8. **WHITE COMPRESSED CHARCOAL**

9. **WORKABLE FIXATIVE**

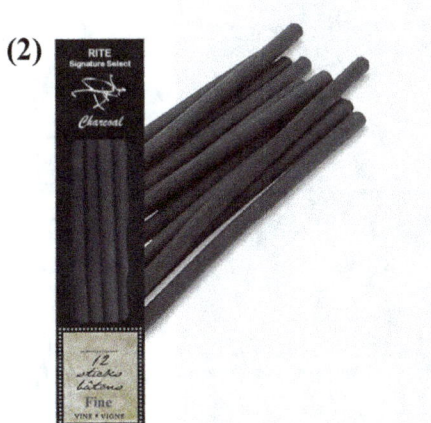

Not actual size of products.
These Images are for entertainment purposes only.
Any similarities to actual products are purely coincidental.

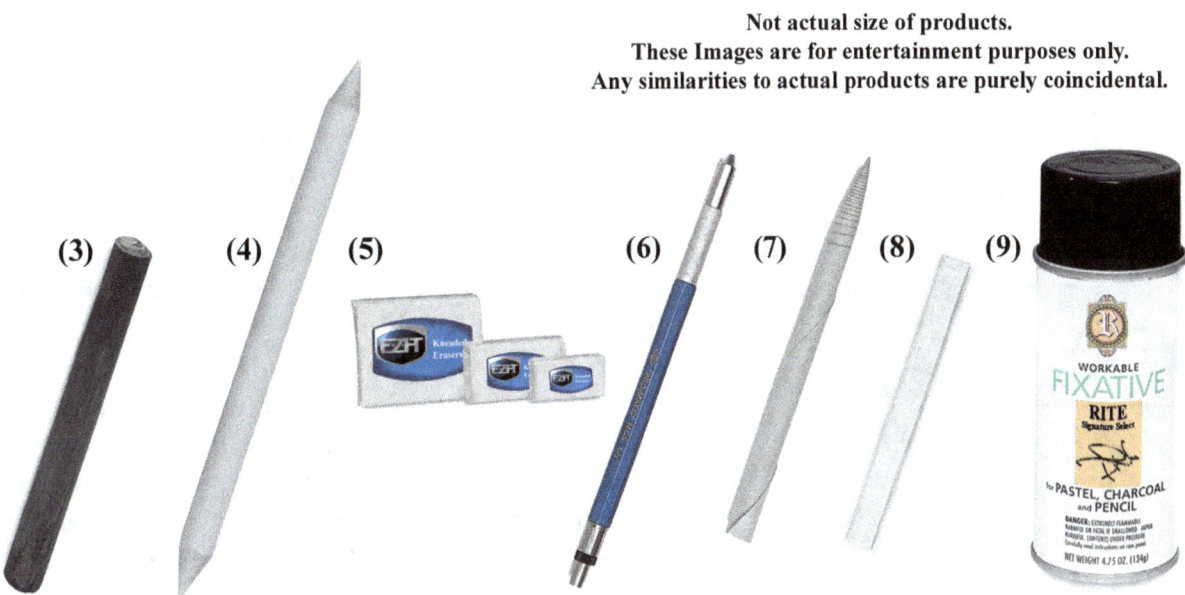

(3) (4) (5) (6) (7) (8) (9)

**You Can Draw Portraits:
Technical Drawing-Mastering an Exact Likeness** *(Introduction)*

THREE-STEP PROCESS

1. OUTLINE
2. MONOCHROME
3. DETAIL

THE OUTLINE

The outline is of particular importance. This is the first step where all the major positions in the work are identified. It is the rendering of the map points in the composition *(as illustrated below)*. These positions will be used as reference points in the drawing.

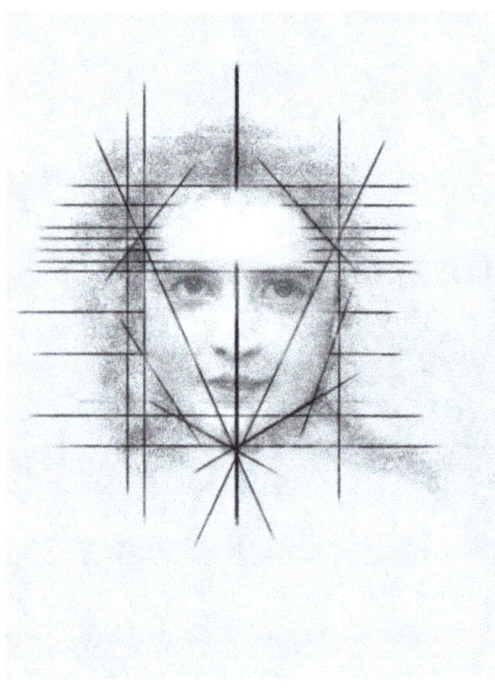

For illustrational purposes, I have darkened in the image *(on the left)* to show how the dark number 9 charcoal lines appear pinpointing where the features are placed. I have chosen a charcoal paper that is thick, with a smooth eggshell type surface, which provides greater detail. There are three reasons that I use the number 9 charcoal stick. First, it keeps the drawing simple, which enables a quick rendition for the following stages. Second, it makes it easier to see the mapping points on the support. Third, the heavy dark vertical, horizontal, and diagonal lines that are used as markers deliver extra charcoal that can be used later for blending and toning. There are different kinds of charcoal paper that are of particular significance. The paper will determine the detail and look of the drawing. Charcoal paper needs a good texture, called tooth *(light and smooth or rough and bumpy)*, as its surface catches the charcoal along the face of the paper which makes for a brilliant image.

THE MONOCHROME

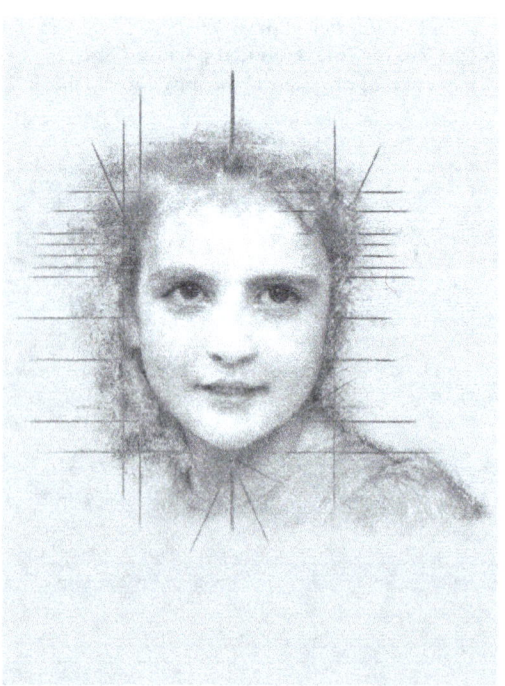

The monochrome stage is the second step in this three-step process that is rendered to find all the subtle tonal values in the drawing. There are a few steps within the monochrome stage. First, is defining the facial features. Second, is restating the facial features using the grayscale. The goal is to render the tonal values as a light version of the portrait that will be detailed *(or darkened)* in the later stages of the drawing. The last step, is finding and correcting any mistakes. We will be using the white charcoal, kneaded erasers, and stumps to smooth and blend the material to make these corrections. This prepares us for the next and final stage of the portrait, the detail.

You Can Draw Portraits:
Technical Drawing-Mastering an Exact Likeness *(Introduction)*

THE DETAIL

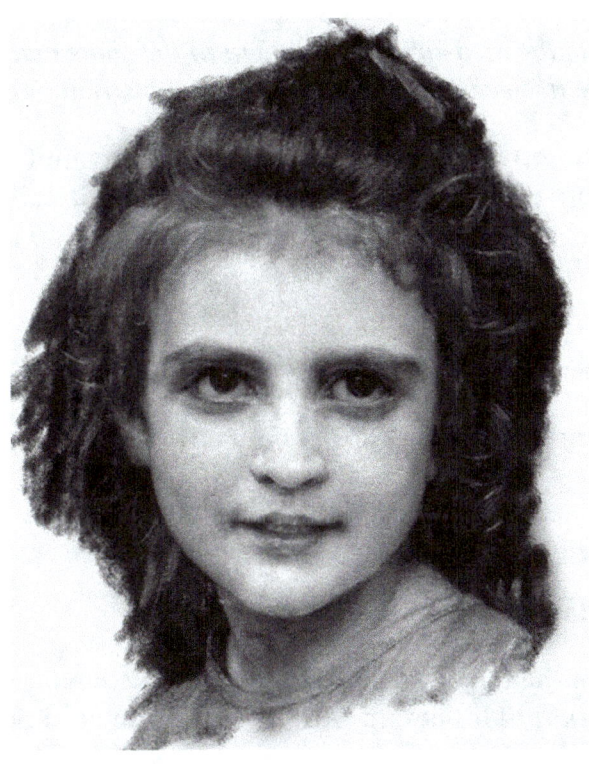

It has been my experience that in the third step, the details of the drawing, is the most satisfying stage. It is in this step where each variation of the drawing comes to life. We have already identified all the important mapping points in the drawing from the previous steps. Now it is a matter of enjoying and restating those points using the correct tonal values.

The tonal values from the light sources are what gives the work texture, interest, and life. It is at this stage we need to make sure to check for the direction of the main light, reflected light, and the highlights. We also need to check the accuracy of the deep shadows and cast shadows.

It will take time to develop the eye and hand coordination to master the skill of draftsmanship.

Nevertheless, do not become discouraged or overwhelmed. Just as you would not expect to pick up a violin and play like a virtuoso and so you should not expect to pick up a pencil and draw like a master artisan. Here is a little excerpt from a story that might help illustrate this point. It was during a classical concert, a violinist stood up and played a solo piece that thrilled the audience. After the concert was over the soloist was approached by a man that complemented the violinist on her talent and said, *"I'd give up half of my life if I could play like that"* to which she replied, *"I did"*.

The good news is, that it will not take half of your life to learn how to draw. Inasmuch, as the fundamentals are not as complicated as learning how to play the violin. It will take time practicing the techniques that you will be learning here that will eventuate in a drawing as pleasing to the eye as a concerto is to the ears.

"Art is not a treasure in the past or an importation from another land, but part of the present life of all living and creating peoples."

~ Franklin D. Roosevelt

You Can Draw Portraits:
Technical Drawing-Mastering an Exact Likeness *(Introduction)*

THE 12-STEP FORMULA

In the following formula, remember to always hold the measuring instrument in the same place or position each time you measure a facial feature (if needed, place a mark on the instrument).

Listed below are 12-steps that I refer to as the 12-Step Formula for drawing. Keep in mind these steps as you perform the drawing techniques in the Outline, Monochrome, and Detail stages *(the three-step process)* in this book.

They are as follows:

01. Grip the measuring instrument in your fist leaving the thumb free.

02. Hold your arm out straight with the thumb and measuring instrument sticking straight up. *(As seen on page 19)*

03. Mark the top of the drawing *(top hair limit line)* by placing a horizontal limit line.

04. Mark the bottom of the chin with a horizontal limit line.

05. Close one eye and measure the distance from the top of the head to the chin by moving your thumb up *(the measurement instrument)* until it lines up with the center point of the subject's head.

06. Now that you have found the top and bottom horizontal limit lines, draw a horizontal line to mark the halfway point axis.

07. Now hold that measurement from the top of the measuring instrument to the thumb and line it up with the bottom of your last measurement to find their halfway points, then mark them.

08. As you have divided the top and bottom horizontal limit lines in half, now place a vertical line that is perpendicular in the center of the horizontal limit lines. This becomes the center vertical axis point, of your subject.

09. Repeat this process for all of the horizontal and vertical points, dividing in half, and marking those reference points.

10. This will give you the overall length of the head and will be the foundation for the facial reference mapping points.

11. Vertical lines are used in the same manner as the horizontal lines to mark the starting and ending points on the subject's features.

12. Diagonal angles are used in conjunction with the horizontal and vertical lines to shape angles that are transferred to your work.

Each of these steps will be illustrated in the following sections.

DRAWING WITH CONFIDENCE:
Section: 2

"Whatever the mind of man can conceive and believe, it can achieve."

~ Napoleon Hill

DRAWING WITH CONFIDENCE

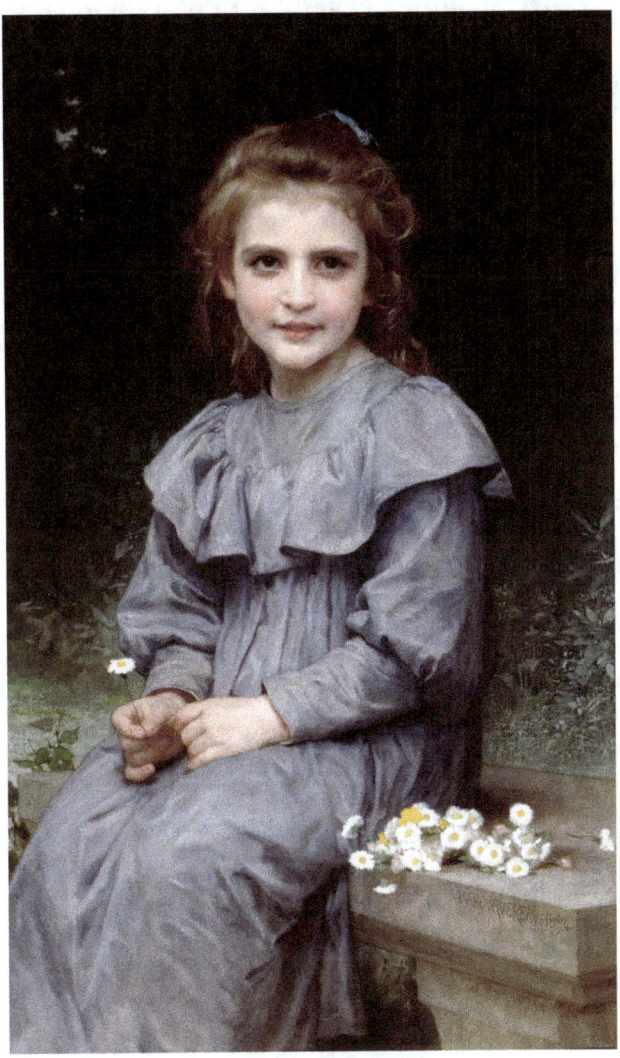

"Daisies" By William Adolphe Bouguereau (1894)

Although their advice was sincere and well-intended, I knew that there had to be drawing and painting techniques that were based upon exacting principles that could systematically guarantee an accomplished work for everyone willing to learn them.

I found those principles existed in the classical traditions and were taught in the schools of a bygone era. One only must go to a museum, where classical paintings are displayed, to view and feel their timeless inspiration. Within these pages, I will share with you the principles of drawing that I have discovered which were used by the master draftsmen from the enduring classical traditions.

Drawing presents a challenge for most beginners if not all of us. Even those that have drawn for a long time know that drawing can be frustrating, especially if their emotions enter the equation. Intermediate to advanced students that draw understand the difficulty that can arise when trying to draw subjects with an exact likeness.

In order to draw with confidence and accuracy the masters knew that one's emotions needed to be taken out of the equation. So, they developed the rules of draftsmanship that excluded emotions from the process.

I have always had a natural love for drawing and painting. Even so, when I first started to enjoy the visual arts as a productive and relaxing hobby, I did not know that there was much more to it than simply picking up a pencil or brush and hope that I would be able to get a reasonable result. As I searched for guidance, I found that every artist and teacher had a different opinion about the best artistic techniques to apply to get the expected result that I was hoping for.

Everything from historical and contemporary styles to doing "just what comes natural" was suggested to me. I found that I was more confused after asking questions on how to obtain the results that I desired than I had been before.

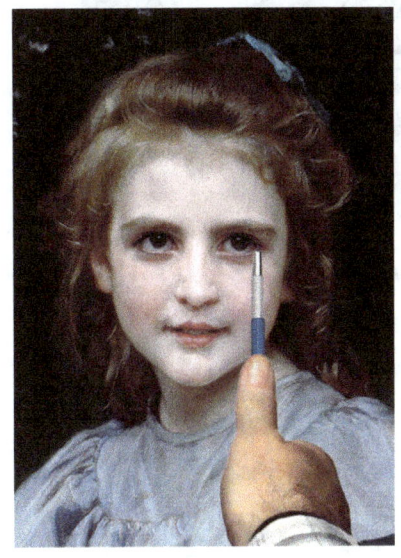

You Can Draw Portraits:
Technical Drawing-Mastering an Exact Likeness *(Drawing with Confidence)*

Drawing accurately depends upon certain points corresponding exactly with other points on the canvas. Thus, the use of a measuring instrument was used for measuring, comparing, and orientating drawing points *(see 12-Step Formula)*. As these points were marked upon the canvas, they eventually made an outline, or a road map, for the artist to follow.

Additionally, a generalization or standard of proportions for the perfect form was devised. This was to aid the artist in understanding the ideal form as a starting point on which to build.

THE STANDARD PROPORTIONS

The eyes are halfway between the top of the head and the chin.

The bottom of the nose is halfway between the eyes and the chin.

The mouth is halfway between the nose and the chin.

The corners of the mouth line up with the center of the eyes.

The top of the ears will line up above the eyes, on the eyebrows.

The bottom of the ears will line up with the bottom of the nose.

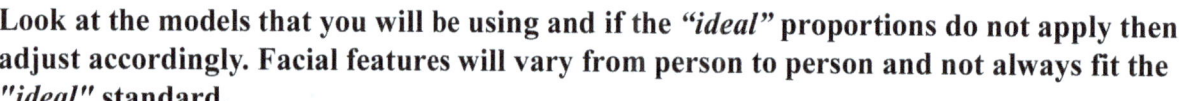

Look at the models that you will be using and if the *"ideal"* proportions do not apply then adjust accordingly. Facial features will vary from person to person and not always fit the *"ideal"* standard.

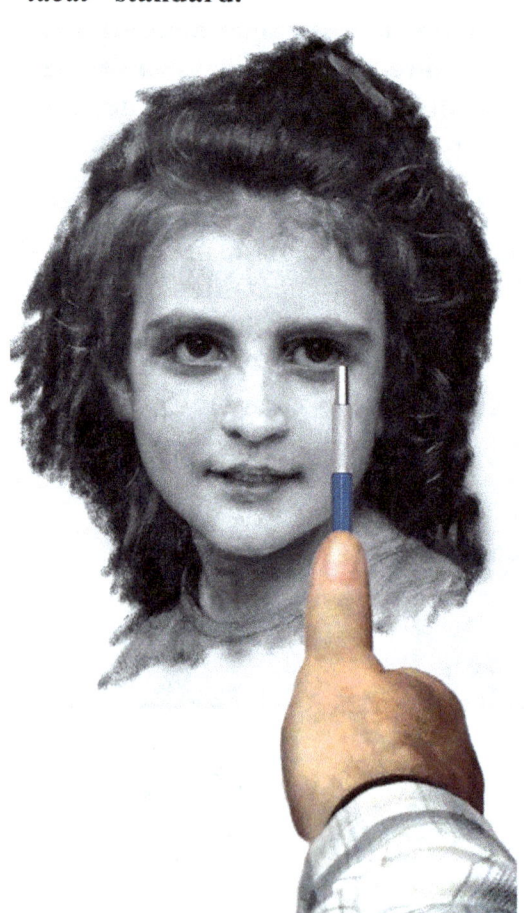

We will begin the portrait by using a charcoal number 9 stick and drawing on charcoal paper. While drawing, notice some remarkably interesting characteristics of the charcoal's additive and subtractive nature. Charcoal is known as a subtractive material, that is, it is a drawing medium that is first added or applied onto a support *(paper or canvas etc.)* then subtracted by smearing and/or erasing to obtain gradations of gray using the paper as the lightest shade.

For example, when the shape of a mark or smear is not correct *(the smear's tones are inaccurate)*, a drawing eraser *(known as a kneaded eraser)* is then applied to subtract the material. One may also use a stump, fingers, or any other aid to get the desired result.

This process of using the black of the charcoal as the darkest tone and the support as its opposite, forces the artist to mix the two opposing tones, in order to obtain the remaining variations in the grayscale. This is an important step in training the eye to see the subtle and delicate shifts of light on the subject being rendered.

PERSPECTIVE / COMPOSITION / TONES

PERSPECTIVE

Perspective allows for the principle of foreshortening. Which simply means, that objects far away seem smaller than they really are and the things that are close seem big. There are two types of perspectives that every artist should be aware of. They are the one and two-point perspectives. This means that in the one-point perspective there is only one vanishing point on the horizon. In the second type of perspective there are two vanishing points on the horizon. *(See illustration below)*

The diagonal line going into the vanishing point can represent any object. For instance, in this example of the *one-point perspective*, imagine a fence and a road going into the horizon and vanishing away. In the *two-point perspective* example, imagine being at a corner of a building with two vanishing points.

The one-point and two-point perspectives:

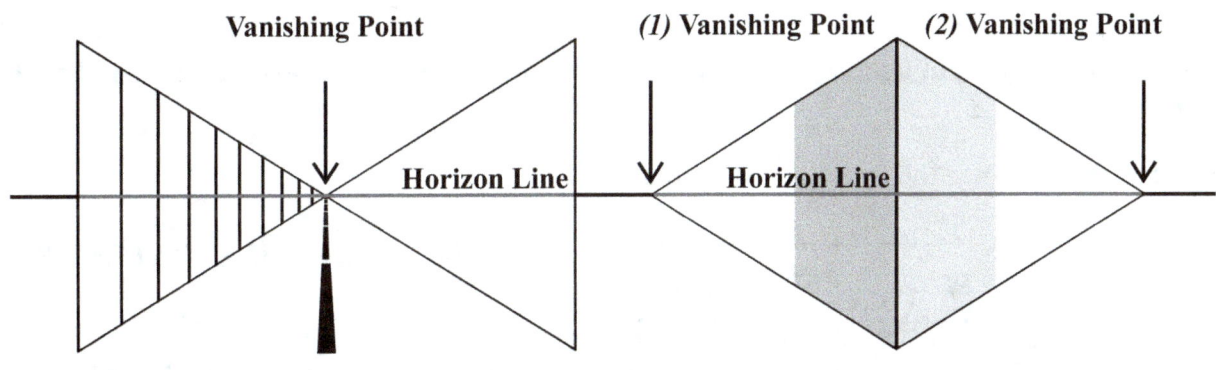

COMPOSITION

I could write a whole book on the importance and purpose of composition because it is essential to the viewing audience. This is a quick introduction to the meaning of composition and how it relates to art. A composition is a form of telling a story on a support. It is judged to be good, bad, or mediocre by the way the subjects, objects, and colors are arranged. The artist should ask, *"Is there a flow to the composition that the eye can easily follow and lead the observer into the subject matter? Or do the objects and color in the work compliment the subject matter?"*

TONES

A tone refers to the degree of lightness or darkness of an area. The tones vary from the bright white of a light source through shades of gray to the deepest black shadows. Tones are the subtle variations of the grayscale that shift from light to dark. The drawing material is applied to the surface or support, which create the delicate variation of the grayscale. *(See page 135 Glossary for the grayscale.)*

**You Can Draw Portraits:
Technical Drawing-Mastering an Exact Likeness**   *(Drawing with Confidence)*

LIGHTS AND SHADOWS

THINGS YOU SHOULD KNOW

In a drawing the lights and shadows play an integral part in turning a one-dimensional object into a three-dimensional existence. Light plays an essential part in a drawing. Textures of an object can be discovered as the surface is revealed by the light bouncing off it.

In the example below, a light strikes the apple. This light shining upon the object is called the main light source or direct light *(C)*. As the light passes around the object, notice the apple's shadow *(A)*, directly opposite of the main light source. The point upon which the direct light first illuminates the object is the brightest point on the surface texture; this point is called the highlight *(E)*.

Then notice a subtitle light shaping the outside of the shadow at its darkest point; this is called the reflected light *(D)*. The reflected light is caused either by the main light source bouncing off another object or from a lesser light source.

The main shadow, or the darkest part of the object, has already been observed. The minor shadow that is caused by the object casting its image upon the background is called the cast shadow *(B)*.

Here are three types of lights and two types of shadows that will give texture and detail to the drawing.

Illustrated below are the lights and shadows.

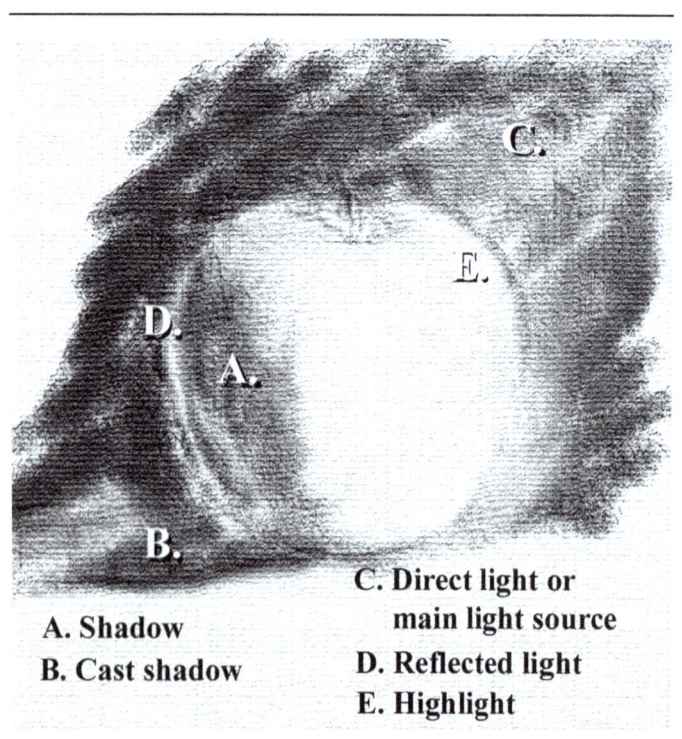

A. Shadow
B. Cast shadow
C. Direct light or main light source
D. Reflected light
E. Highlight

THERE ARE THREE TYPES OF LIGHTS

1. *Main light source (or Direct Light)*

2. *Highlight*

3. *Reflected light*

THERE ARE TWO TYPES OF SHADOWS

1. *Shadow*

2. *Cast Shadow*

18

You Can Draw Portraits:
Technical Drawing-Mastering an Exact Likeness *(Drawing with Confidence)*

As mentioned before drawing accurately depends upon certain points corresponding exactly with other points on the canvas. In the illustration below, is a measuring instrument that I used for orienting, measuring, and comparing drawing points. As these points are marked upon the canvas, they eventually make an outline, or road map, for the artist to follow.

In this text, whenever an illustration is given in reference to the right or left, it is referring to the models right or left.

By specifying the subject's limitations, through the use of limit lines, decide where on the support the image is going to be. There is nothing more frustrating than to draw a wonderful picture only to find out that its placement on the support ruins it. We do not want to just start drawing and as we go along realize that the image is too high, to low, or off to one side and run out of room before the portrait is finished.

THINGS TO REMEMBER

Always keep the arm straight and hold the measuring tool in the exact same way each time a measurement is taken, or significant deformities will occur.

1. **Grip the measuring instrument in your fist leaving the thumb free.**

2. **Hold your arm out straight in a relaxed fashion with the thumb and measuring instrument protruding straight up.**

3. **Make a mark on the top of the drawing by placing what is called a limit line.**

4. **Mark the bottom of your drawing by placing a limit line there also.**

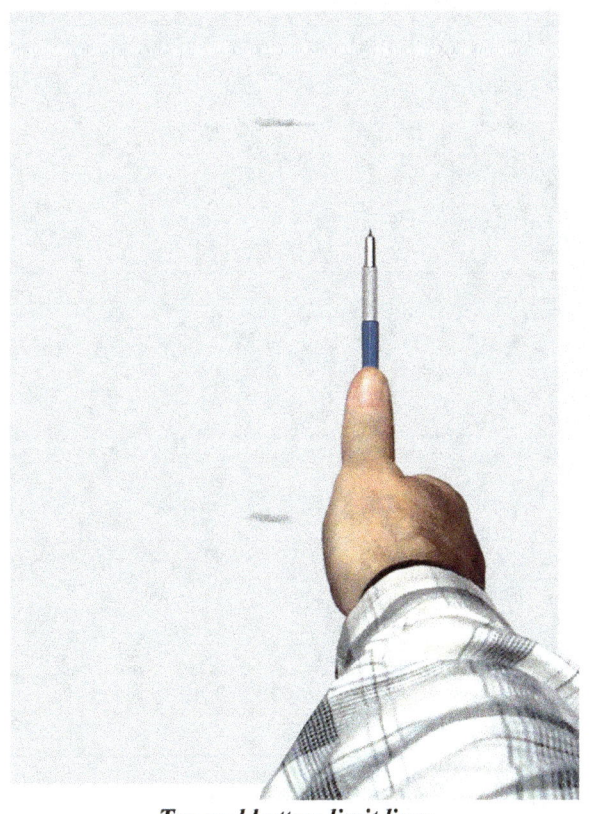

Top and bottom limit lines.

"After all is said and done, more is said than done."

~ Aesop

DRAWING I:
Section: 3

"*A journey of a thousand miles begins with a single step.*"

~ Lao-Tzu

DRAWING I

LETS GET STARTED

Let us now begin with remembering how to hold the measuring instrument, griping the instrument in the fist, leaving the thumb free. While holding the arm out straight, with the instrument in hand *(the mechanical pencil, and from here on I will refer to the measuring instrument, as a pencil)*. Start the drawing as illustrated below.

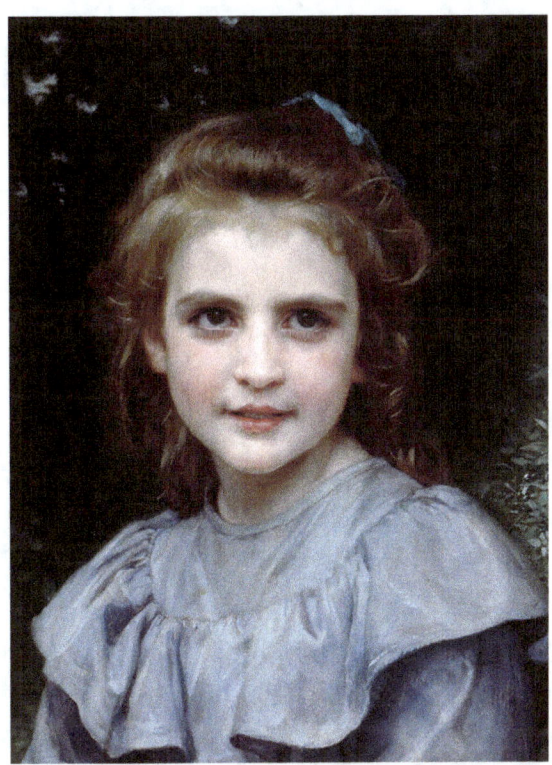

Close one eye and measure the distance from the top of the canvas to where the top of the hair is to be, then mark a limit line. Next, measure from the top of the hair to the chin, by moving your thumb up the pencil until it lines up with the chin. Mark the bottom of the chin with a limit line.

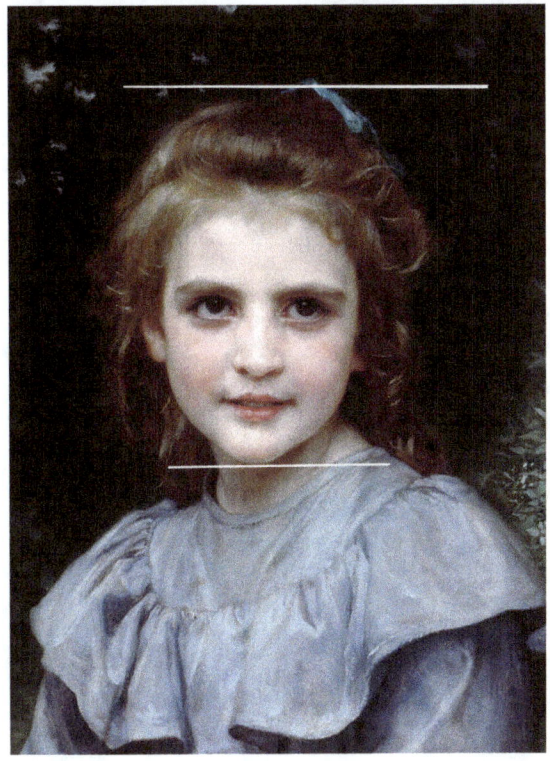

NOTE: The white lines shown in the illustrations (to the left) are imaginary lines that the artist sees to help identify where they are looking to mark the road map on the support. In order to give a better view of the drawing process the following images are close ups of the actual process. See the Appendix as reference to the road map lines.

You Can Draw Portraits:
Technical Drawing-Mastering an Exact Likeness *(Drawing I)*

The brightest white line *(to the left)* is what is currently being demonstrated, unless otherwise noted, we are then marking that line *(to the right)* on the support. The other faded white lines are points that should have already been identified and marked on the canvas. The canvas should look like the support shown to the right. If, however, there is a line represented on the left that is not on the support, review previous illustrations or continue to divide the lines until the point is found on the canvas.

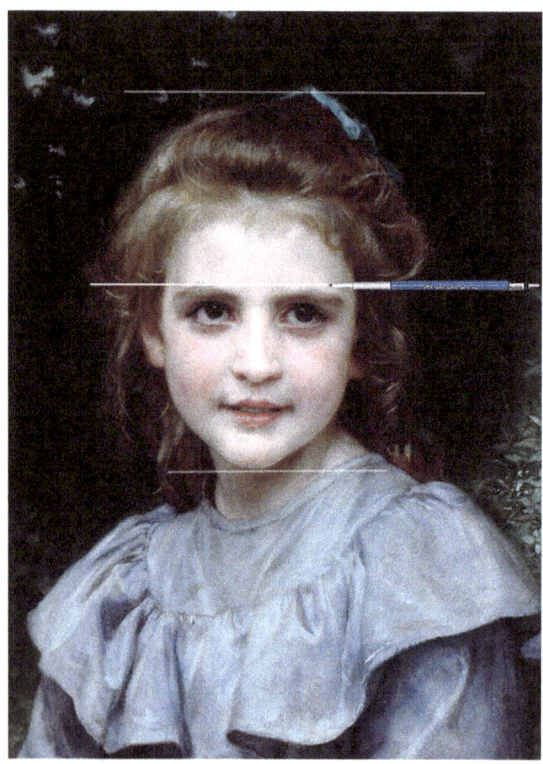

Divide the top and bottom limit lines in half with a *horizontal line* marking the halfway point axis.

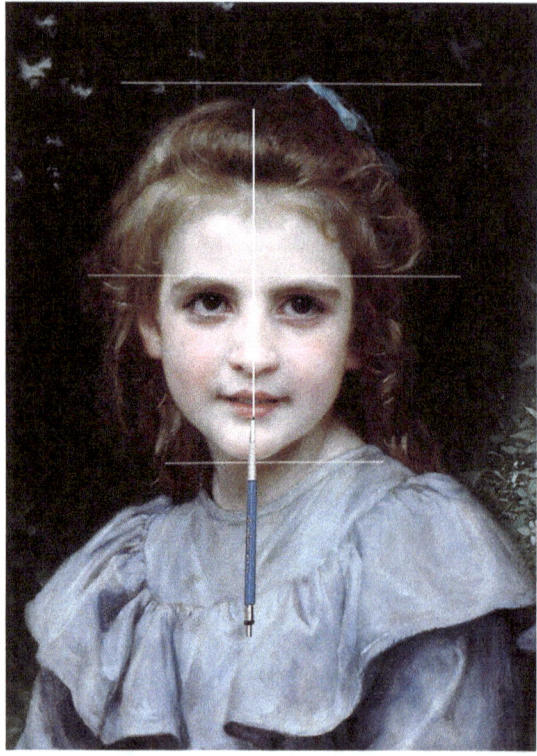

Divide the top and bottom limit lines in half with a vertical line in the center marking the *vertical line* axis point.

You Can Draw Portraits:
Technical Drawing-Mastering an Exact Likeness *(Drawing I)*

FINDING THE MAP POINTS FOR THE WIDTH OF THE FACE

To find the width of the face continue marking the road map points.

Diagonal measurements are used in conjunction with the vertical and horizontal lines to shape angles that are then transferred to the support. Be as accurate as possible in transferring the angles onto the work.

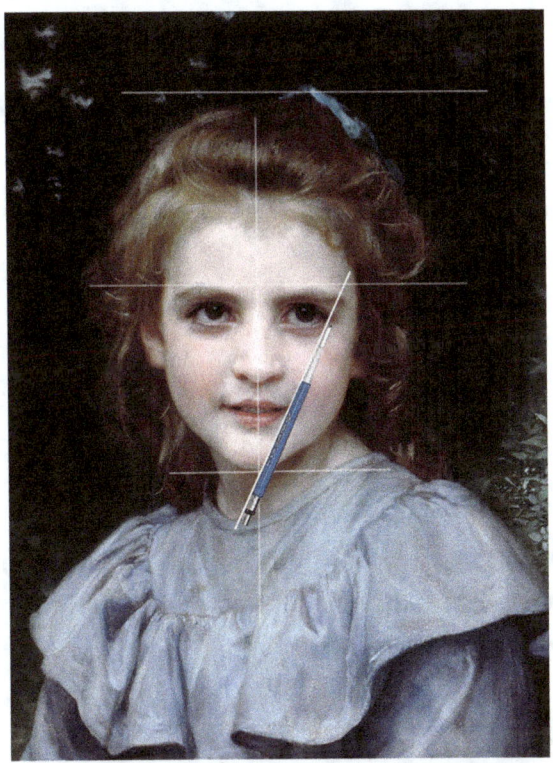

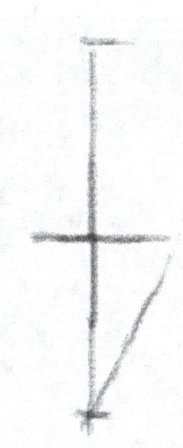

We are looking at both pictures on the left. Draw diagonal lines on the outside of each eye starting from the horizontal chin line to the horizontal brow line. These measurements will help in finding the outside of each cheek.

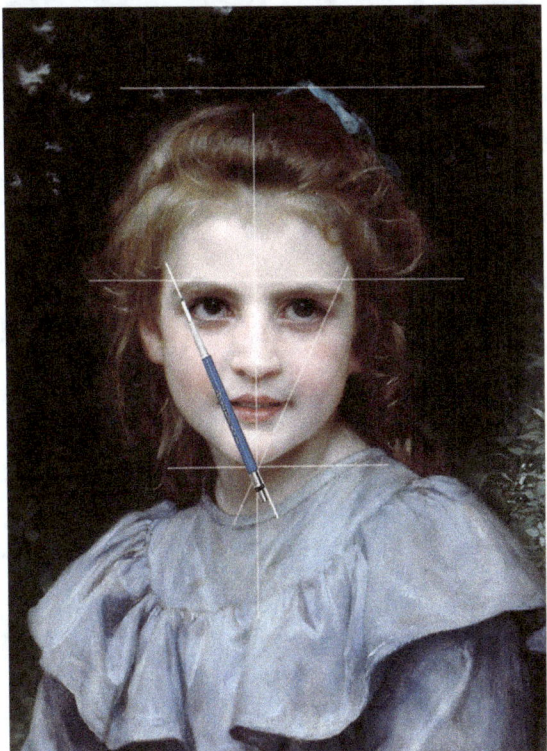

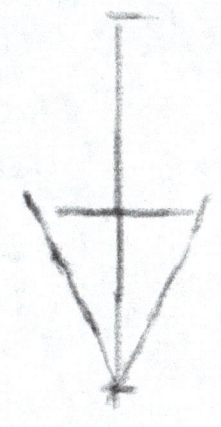

If you do not get it right the first time do not get discouraged, as somone said, *"If you're not erasing, you're not learning"*.

You Can Draw Portraits:
Technical Drawing-Mastering an Exact Likeness *(Drawing I)*

The top and bottom horizontal limit lines have been divided in half with a horizontal line above the eyebrow. Use the brow line and the chin line to find the halfway point which will be the tip of the nose. Mark this point with a horizontal line. *(As illustrated below)*

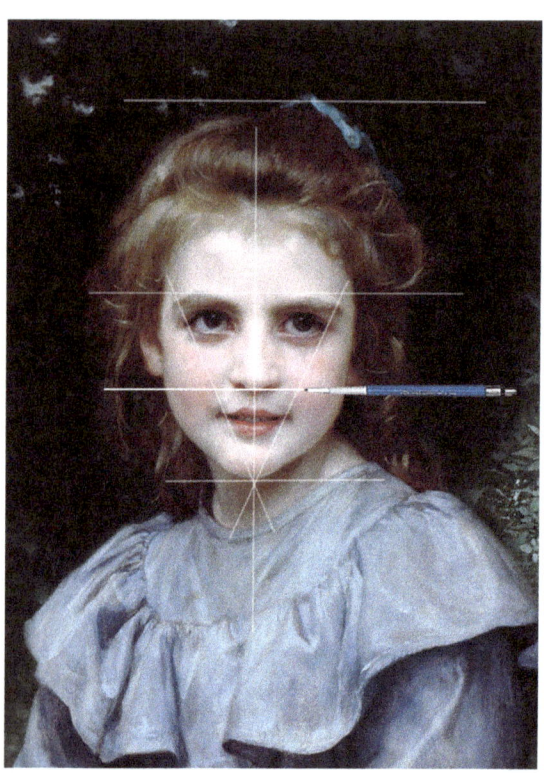

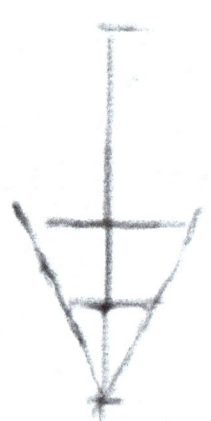

This process will be repeated for all the horizontal mapping points *(dividing in half and marking those reference points)*.

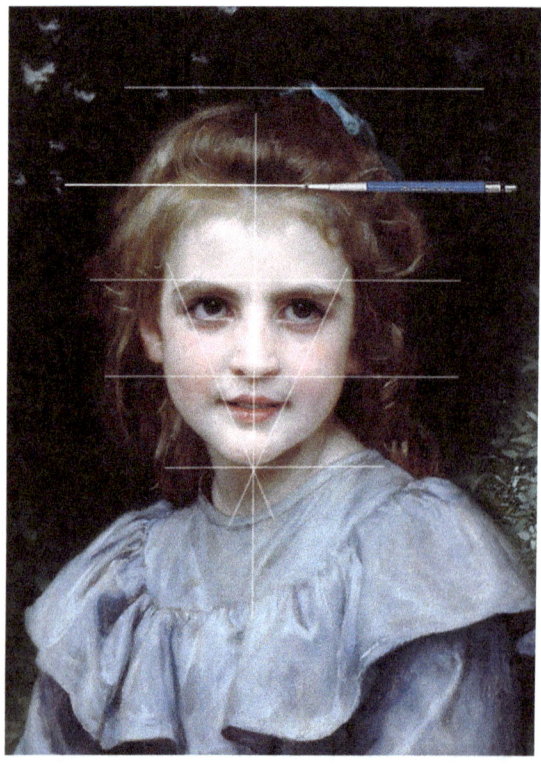

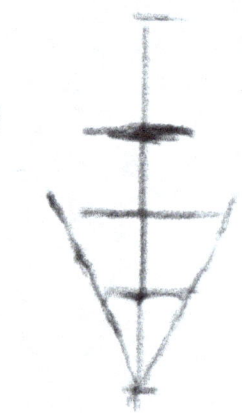

Find the top of the hairline by using this process of dividing each horizontal section into halves.

**You Can Draw Portraits:
Technical Drawing-Mastering an Exact Likeness**   *(Drawing I)*

Dividing the horizontal points in half, and marking those reference points, continue to repeat this process for all the horizontal points as seen below.

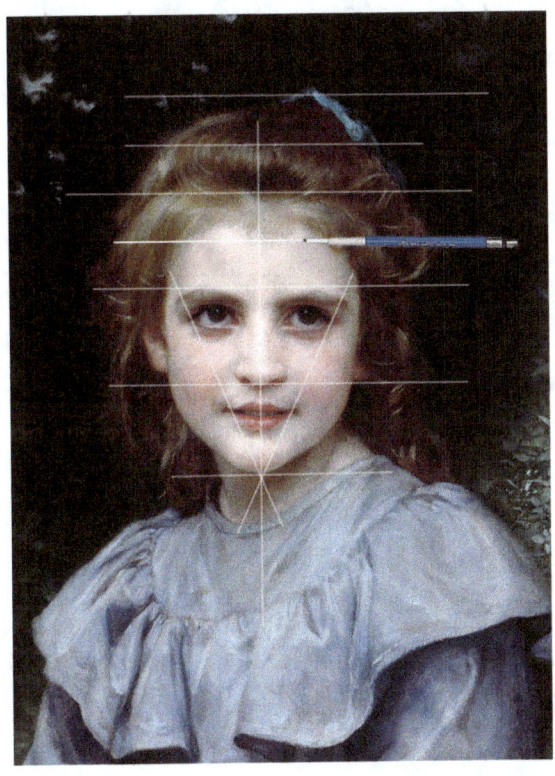

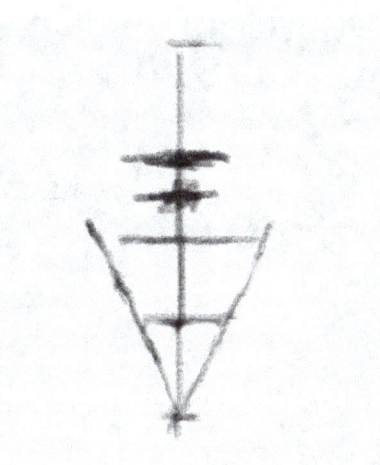

Here the bangs come down from the hairline which is halfway between the hairline and the brow line.

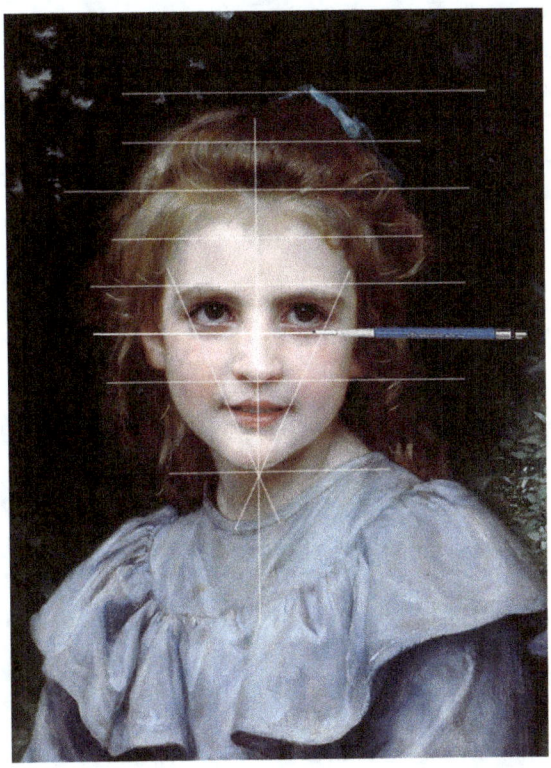

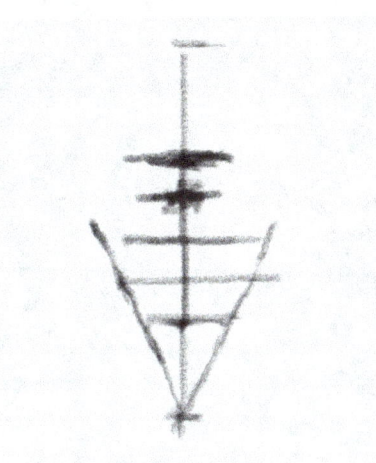

Now find the middle of the nose, which is just under the eyes, half way between the brow and the tip of the nose.

You Can Draw Portraits:
Technical Drawing-Mastering an Exact Likeness   (Drawing I)

Having marked each of the horizontal steps on the canvas or support the work should look like the illustrations below.

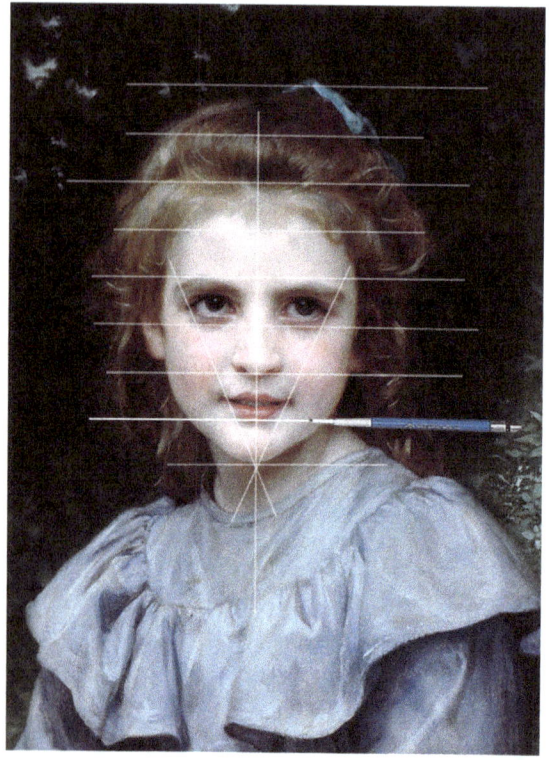

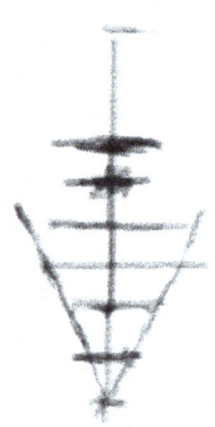

To find the bottom of the mouth and lips go halfway between the tip of the nose and the bottom of the chin. Place a horizontal line.

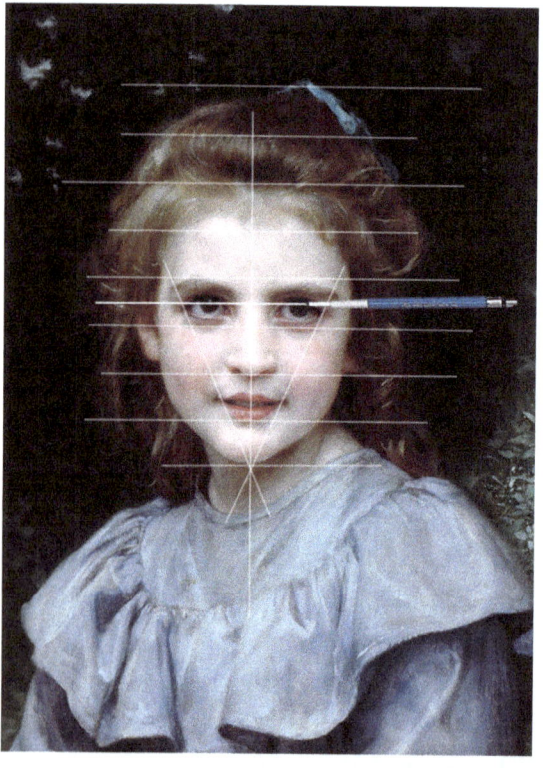

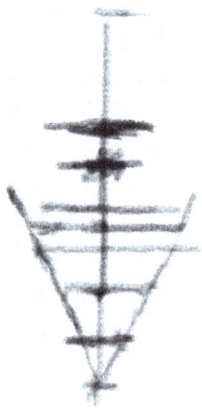

To find where the top of the subject's eyes are located, go halfway between the brow line and the bottom of the eye. Mark with a line.

Note: Continue using the number 9 charcoal stick as we mark our mapping points. See Introduction page 8.

You Can Draw Portraits:
Technical Drawing-Mastering an Exact Likeness *(Drawing I)*

In the early stages, during and after the outline process, it is important to make certain marks and lines that correspond with the location of the subject's facial features. It is this process that allows for an exact likeness to be rendered. After having established most of the horizontal points, it is time now to mark the vertical lines. As with the horizontal limit lines, the vertical lines are no different in reference to marking and dividing them into halves.

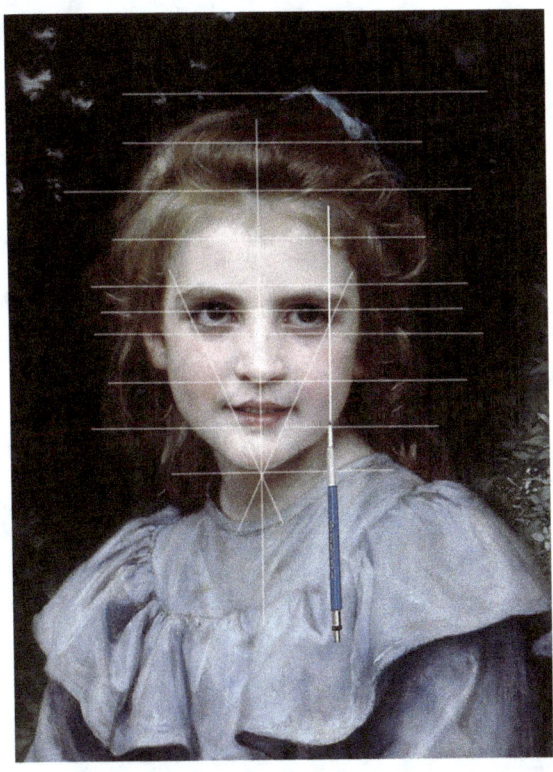

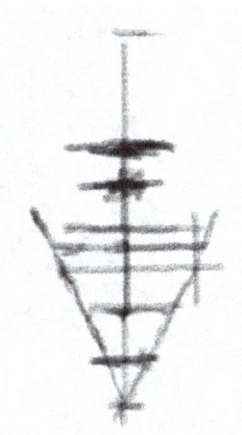

The outside of the left eye is found where the diagonal line meets the outside of the eye. Draw a vertical line up where these two points meet.

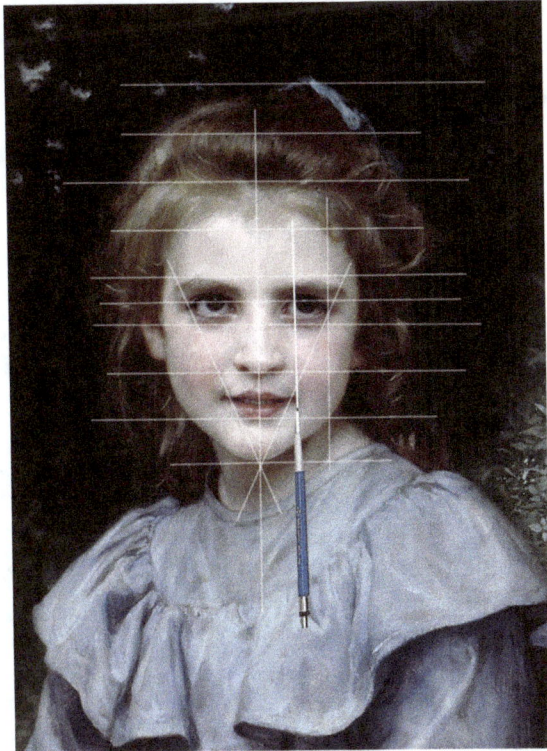

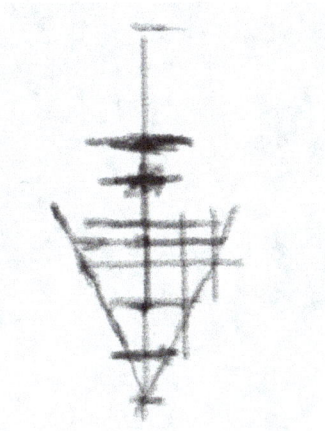

Make a vertical mark by coming in halfway from the vertical line on the left side of the eye and the vertical axis. The vertical line lines up with the iris of the left eye and the corner of the left side of the mouth.

You Can Draw Portraits:
Technical Drawing-Mastering an Exact Likeness   *(Drawing I)*

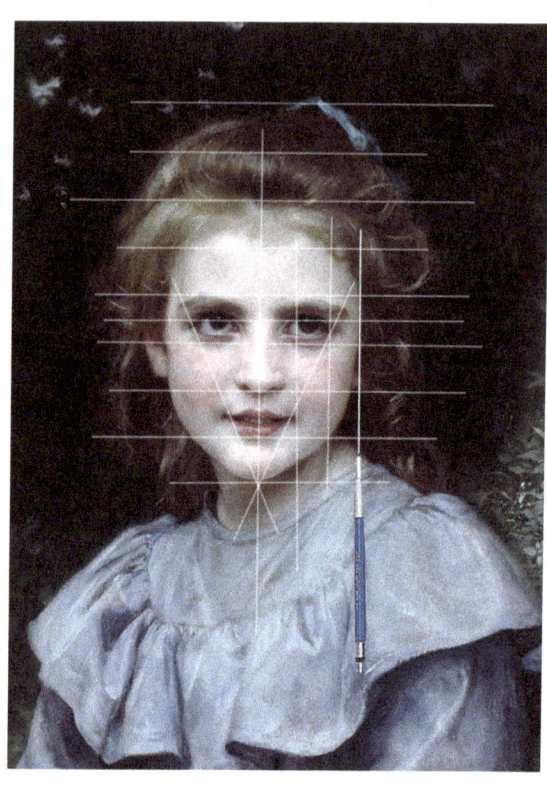

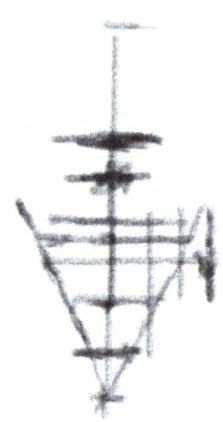

After dividing the outside of the left eye and the vertical axis in half. Now go the same distance outside from the left eye to find the outside left cheek.

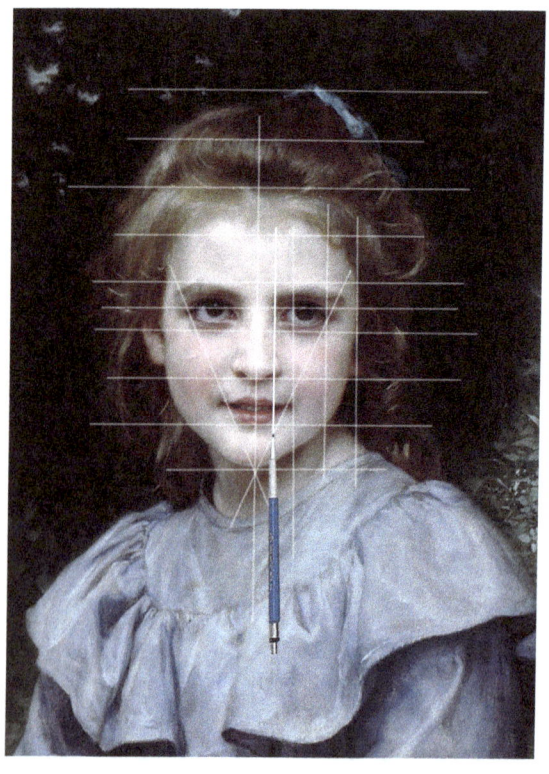

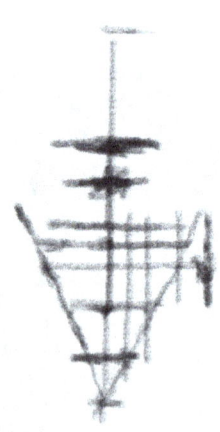

Continue to divide the vertical lines in half to find other important points. Here mark the inside of the left eye, mid nostril, and the lower lip's slope.

You Can Draw Portraits:
Technical Drawing—Mastering an Exact Likeness *(Drawing I)*

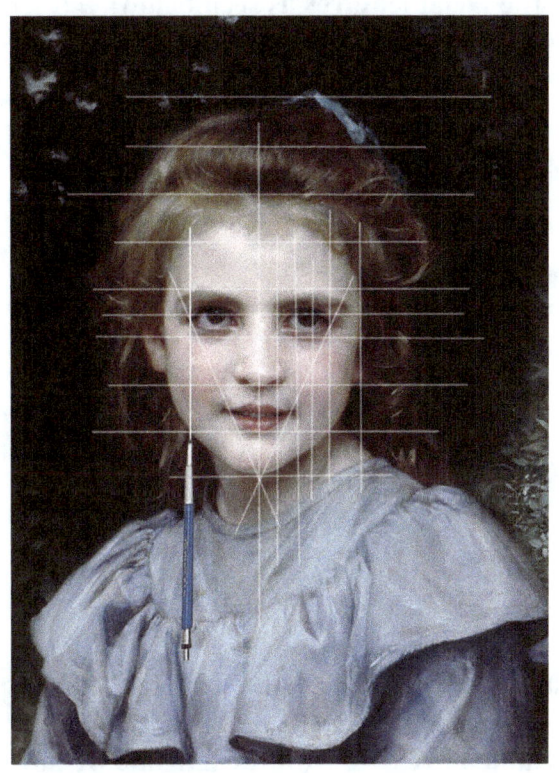

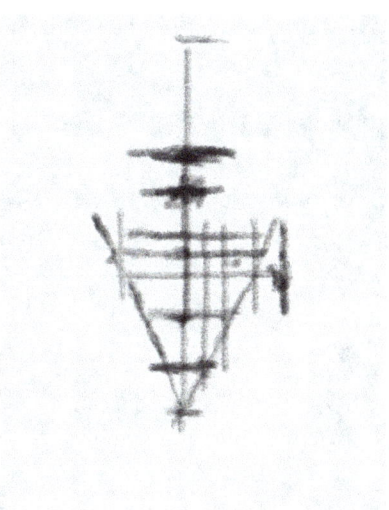

The outside of the right eye is located by repeating the same process as the left eye. Draw a vertical line at the junction point at the diagonal line.

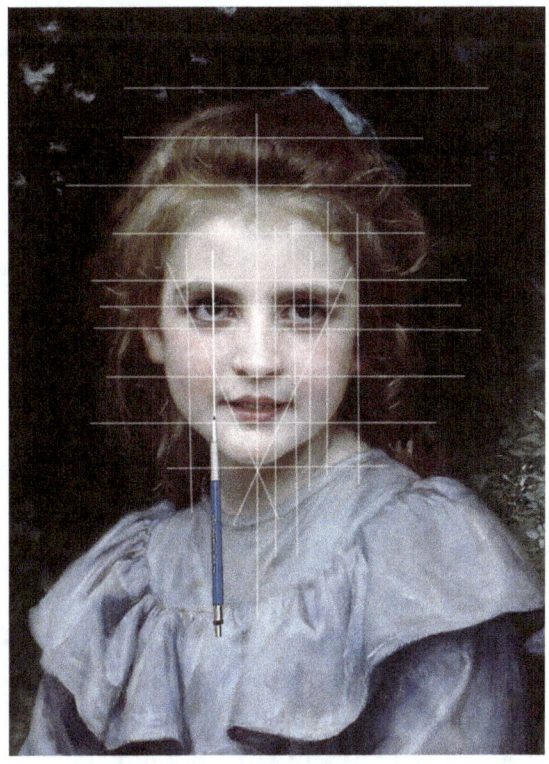

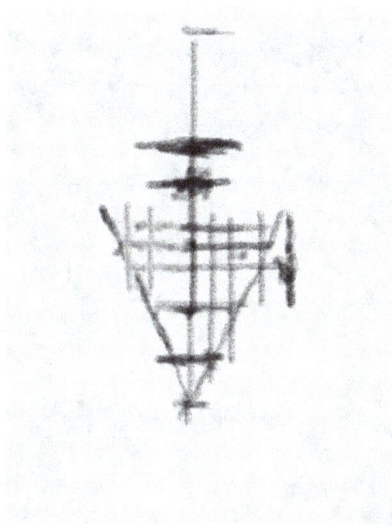

Now mark the middle of the right eye with a vertical line. This line can be found by using the same principle of dividing the halves from the outside vertical line and the vertical axis. Repeat this process three times until the middle of the eye is found.

You Can Draw Portraits:
Technical Drawing-Mastering an Exact Likeness   *(Drawing I)*

Continue to mark the vertical lines by using the horizontal and diagonal lines as markers to know where the starting and ending points are for the facial features as seen below.

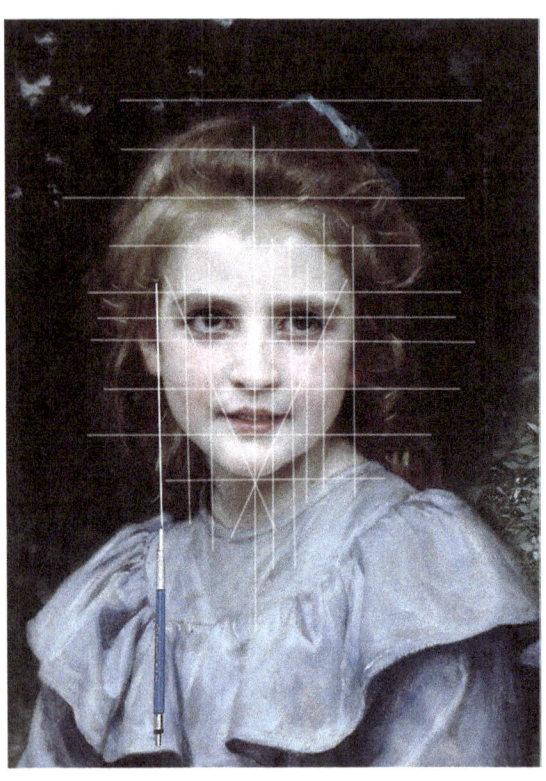

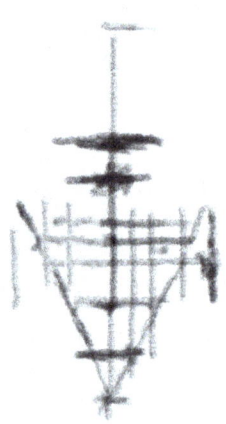

Basically, follow the same format as the left eye, to establish the correct markers for the facial features. As with the left side we now draw a vertical line on the outside of the right cheek.

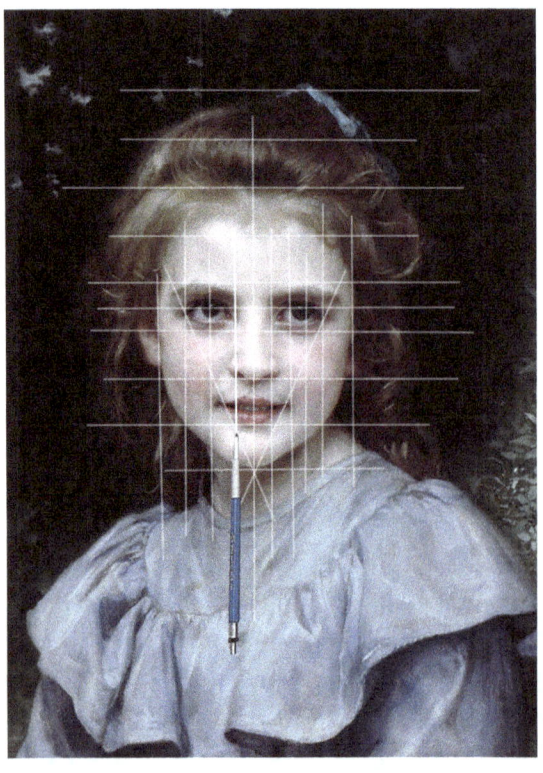

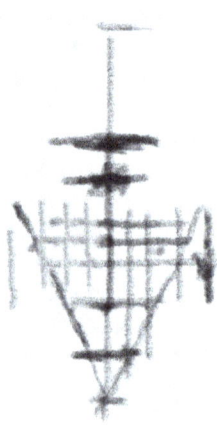

Continue to divide the vertical lines in half to find the inside of the right eye. The canvas should look like the illustration above.

**You Can Draw Portraits:
Technical Drawing-Mastering an Exact Likeness**   *(Drawing I)*

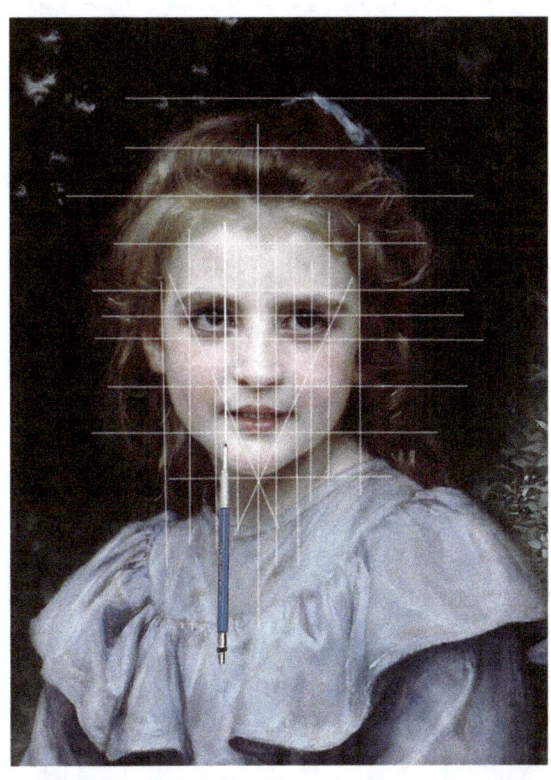

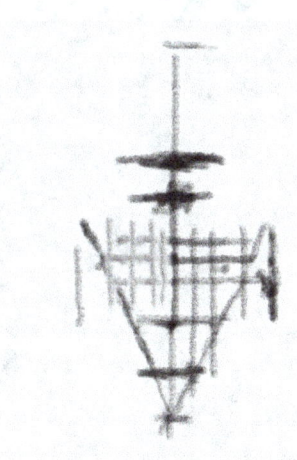

Place a vertical line on the inside of the right iris by dividing the two previous points.

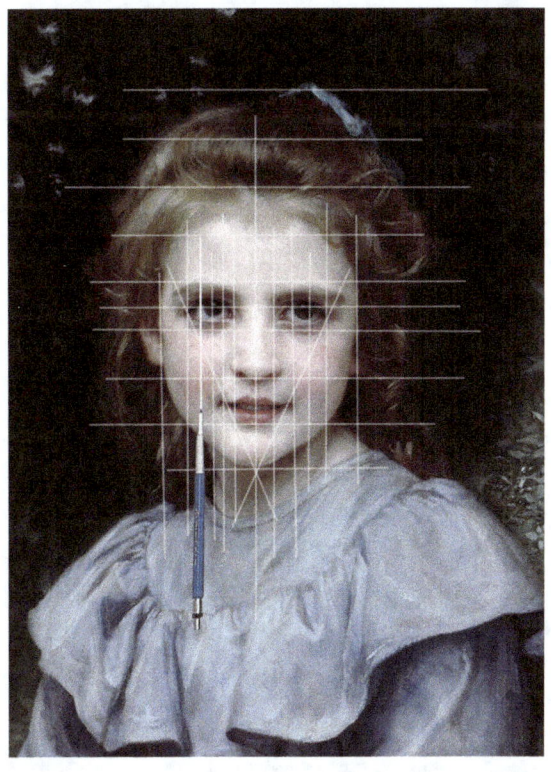

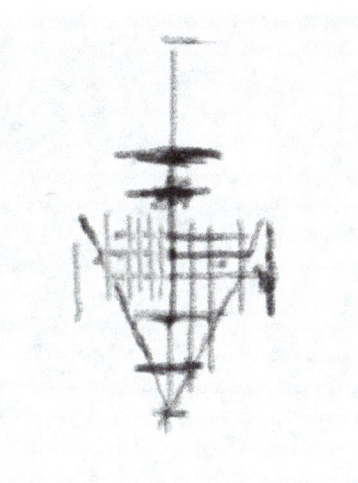

Continue by dividing the right eye's vertical lines in half which places the next vertical point on the outside of the right iris.

NOTE: *At anytime a point cannot be located continue to divide the lines in half until the exact point is found.*

You Can Draw Portraits:
Technical Drawing-Mastering an Exact Likeness *(Drawing I)*

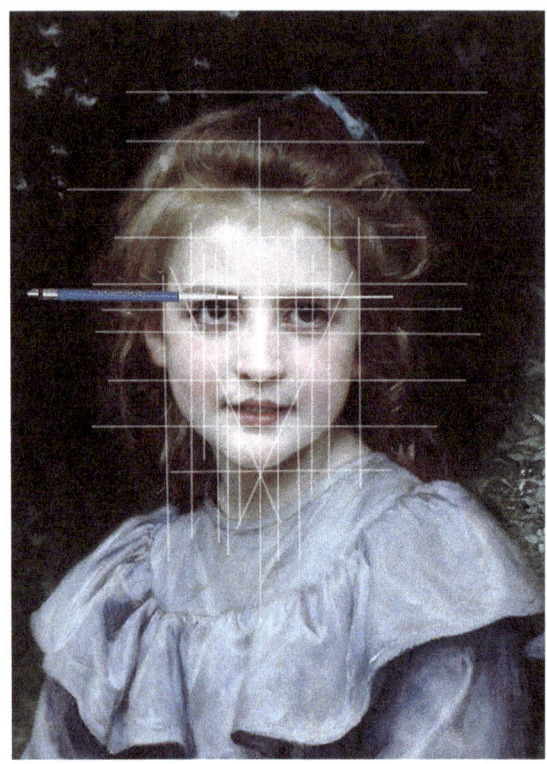

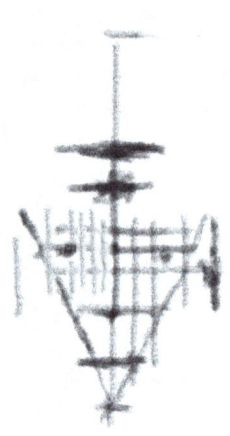

Now divide the top of the eyebrow with the line that runs through the iris to get the bottom of the eyebrow. Place some material to indicate the beginning of the iris.

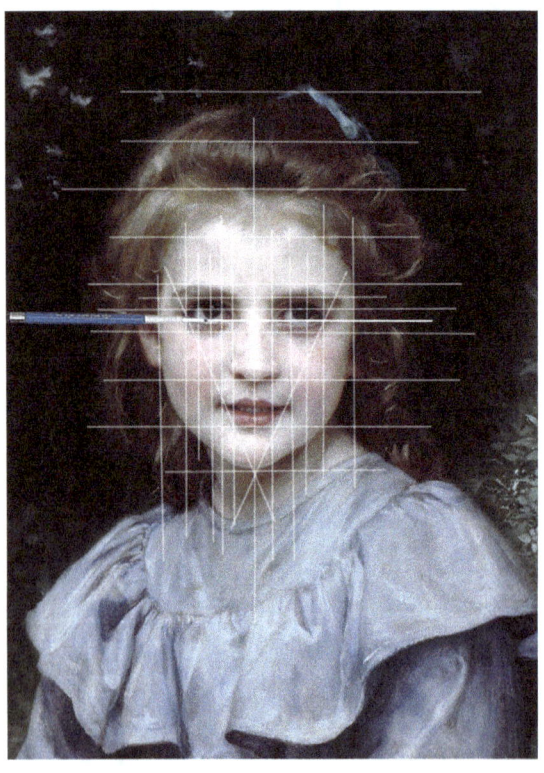

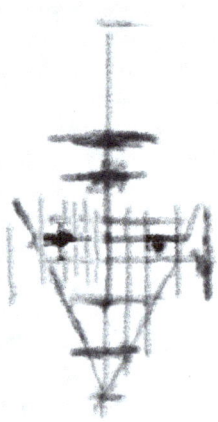

Continue in the same fashion, dividing the horizontal lines to the next horizontal point, which is the top of the bottom eyelids and place a mark.

I like to begin my portraits with the eyes before continuing onto the rest of the facial features. The following section focuses, specifically on the eyes. This step will aid in orienting the rest of the facial features with exact likeness.

DRAWING II:
Section: 4

"*Develop success from failures. Discouragement and failure are two of the surest stepping stones to success.*"

~Dale Carnegie

DRAWING II

DRAWING THE EYES

There is enough information now to start drawing in the eyes. As mentioned briefly in the last section, I always like to start with the eyes, and mostly finish them before going onto the rest of the face. The eyes are the windows to the soul of the individual, so if I get that right, the rest of the face will fall into place quite easily.

The following illustrations are closeup views of each of the steps taken in detail. I only show the left eye's procedure so be sure to use the same process while drawing the right eye. Be sure to draw both eyes at the same time to make sure the placements are exact. Use the remainder of each of the vertical, horizontal, and diagonal lines as placement markers and as blending material.

View the following illustrations from left to right and top to bottom.

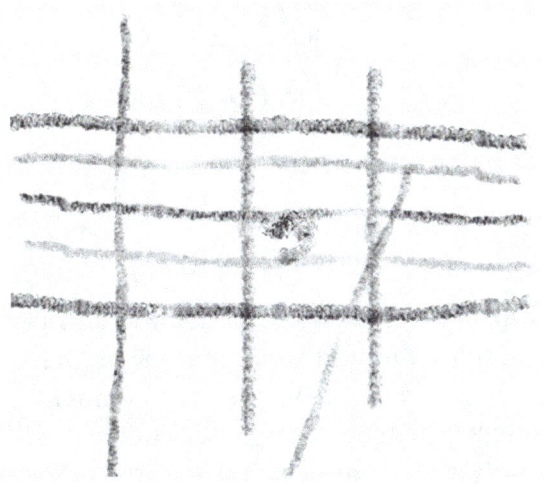

Begin by drawing the iris. To identify its starting point, use the middle of the outside left eye and the center vertical line and place a mark for the iris.

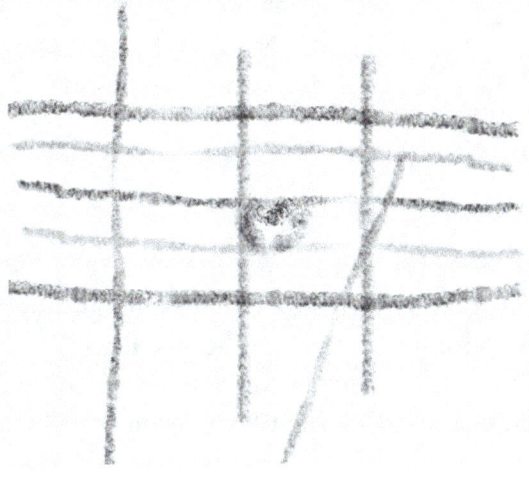

Continue the iris to the horizontal middle point and the horizontal marker below the middle point.

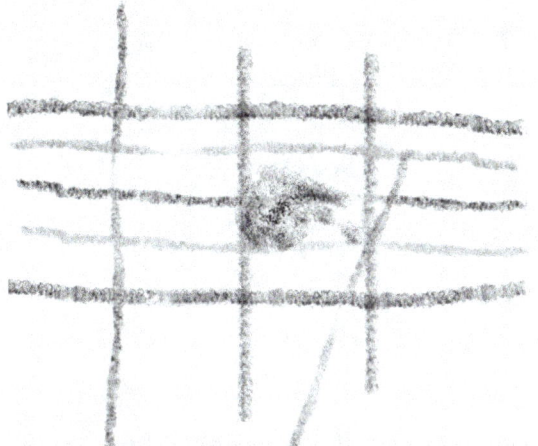

Following the horizontal and middle markers adding the upper eyelid and some shadow. Do not add any detail that will come in later.

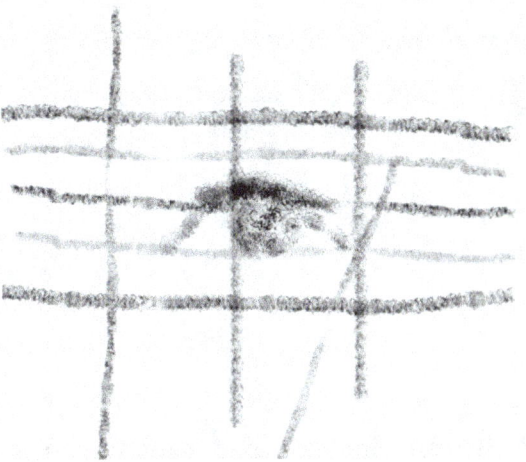

As seen above, draw the upper eyelid and shadow. Using the horizontal markers as a guide.

You Can Draw Portraits:
Technical Drawing-Mastering an Exact Likeness *(Drawing II)*

DRAWING THE EYES

It is very important to draw the right eye at the same time that the left eye is drawn; this will aid in the progress of the work.

Close up of the left eye continued.

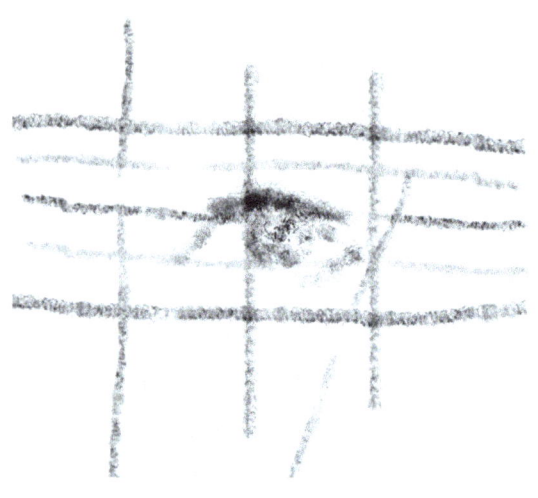

Move on with the lower eyelid by adding some material. Feel free to use the material, remove what is not needed, until the image looks like the illustration.

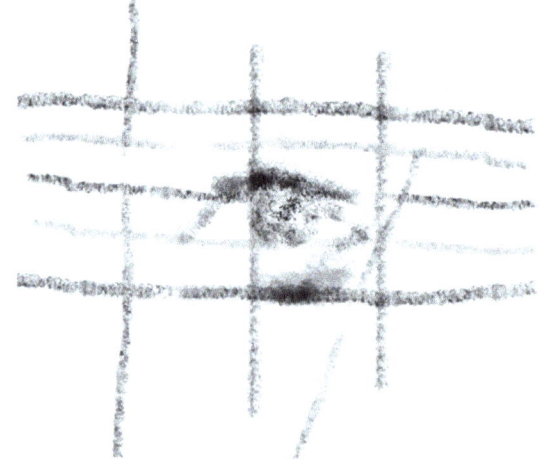

Continue to follow the horizontal and vertical lines and add some shadow on the lower eye muscle. Do not use too much material to avoid being overwhelmed with smudging and/or erasing.

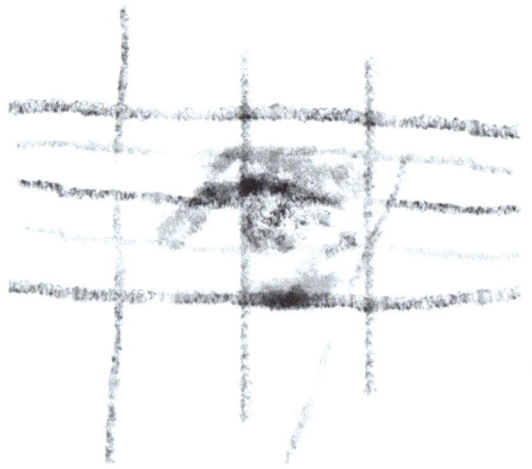

While restating and shadowing the upper lid the eye's location is now well established.

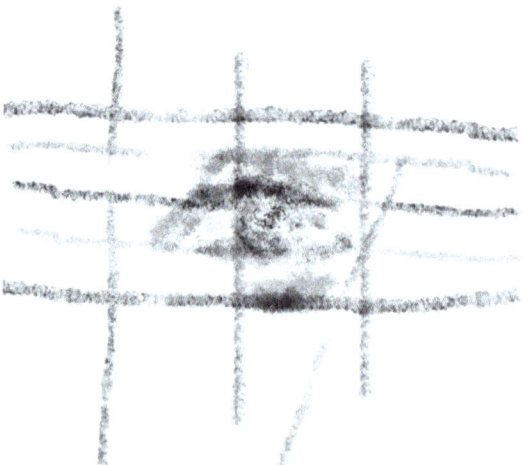

Continue with the lower eyelid matching it up with the horizontal and vertical lines.

**You Can Draw Portraits:
Technical Drawing-Mastering an Exact Likeness** *(Drawing II)*

DRAWING THE EYES

It is very important to draw the right eye at the same time that the left eye is drawn.

Close up of the left eye continued.

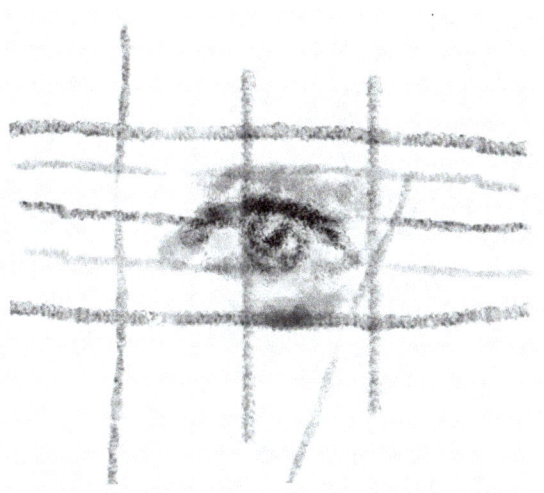

Check the measurements to be sure that the drawing is accurate. Adding more material to darken what has already been stated.

Continue onto the lower eye muscle and add some shadow marking the eye socket.

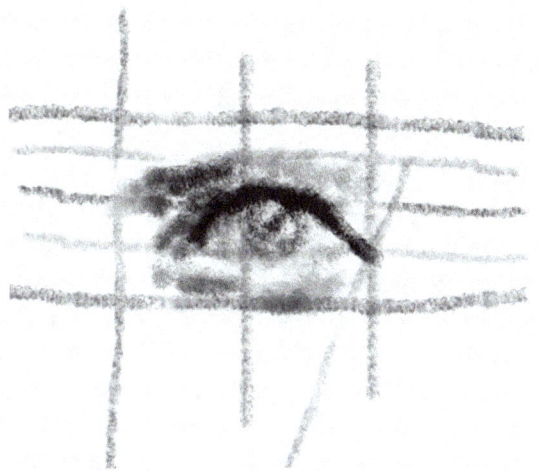
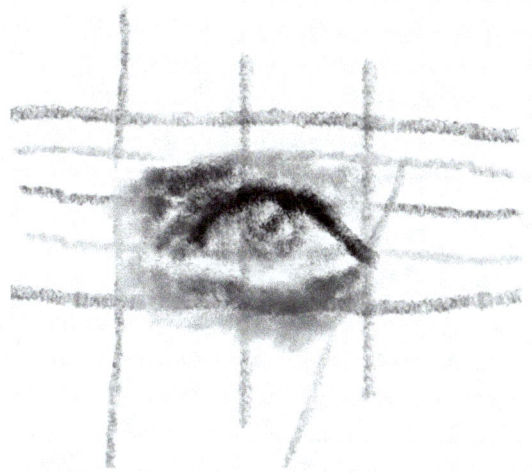

Now restate the upper lid making it darker by adding some contrast while we smooth out the line.

Add some more shadow on the lower muscle.

**You Can Draw Portraits:
Technical Drawing-Mastering an Exact Likeness** *(Drawing II)*

DRAWING THE EYES

It is particularly important to draw the right eye while at the same time the left eye is drawn.

Close up of the left eye continued.

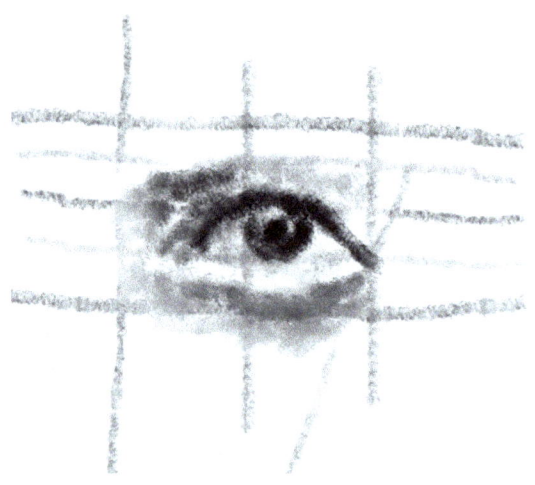

The eye is really starting to take on the look of a real eye. Add more shadow to the iris and rounding it some more.

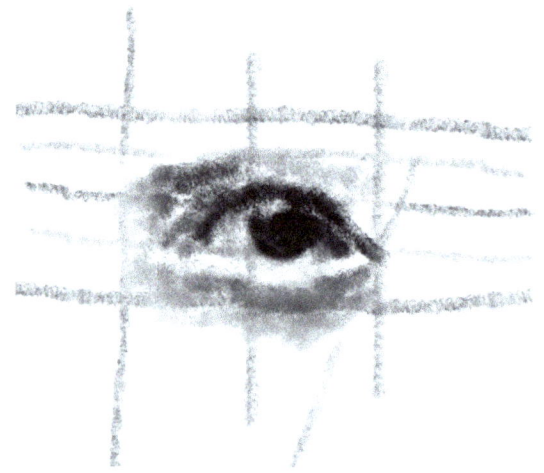

This is exciting! See how the eye is taking shape! Now darken in the iris and add some eye shadow. Then draw a line indicating where part of the upper lid is located.

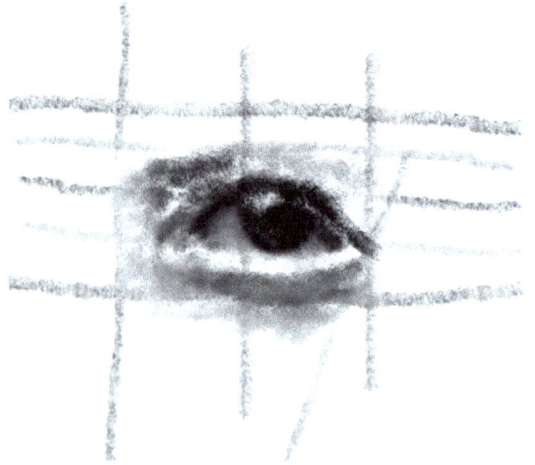

Restate the iris and add some tone to the white of the eyeball.

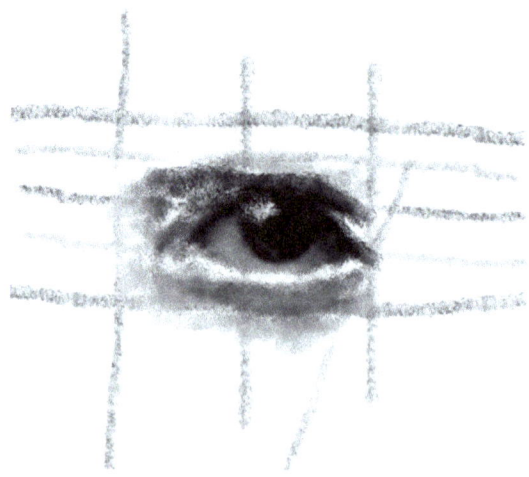

Continue to darken the white of the eye and deepen the shadow on the iris' left side. Notice that the tone of the white part of the eye has shaped the curve of the bottom of the eyelid.

**You Can Draw Portraits:
Technical Drawing-Mastering an Exact Likeness** *(Drawing II)*

DRAWING THE EYES

It is particularly important to draw the right eye while at the same time the left eye is drawn.

Close up of the left eye continued.

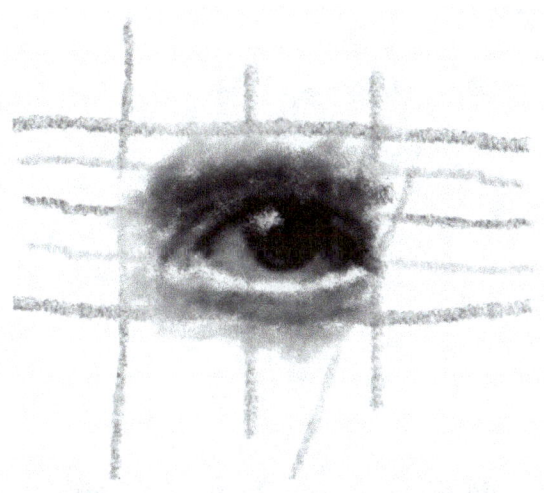

Adding shadow on the upper eye deepens the brow indicating the eye is recessed into its socket.

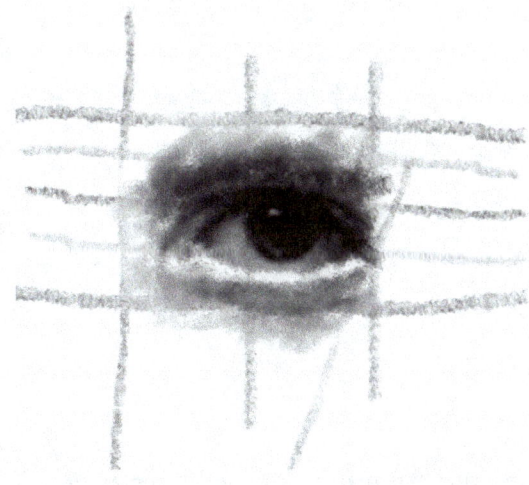

Restate the iris by darkening the pupil leaving an extraordinarily little highlight. Here restate, smooth-out, and fill in the upper lid.

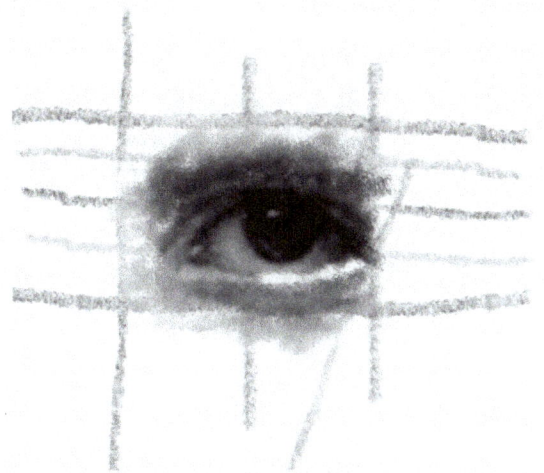

Add some shadow to recess the eyeball and finish the inside corner near the nose. We also add tone to the lower lid's top where it meets the eyeball.

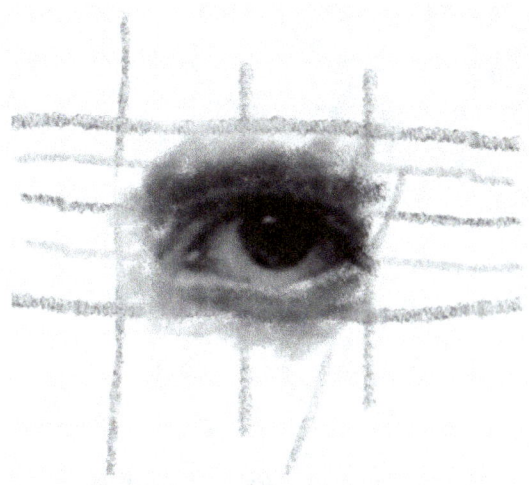

Continue to add tone to the lower lid. The eyes are almost complete.

**You Can Draw Portraits:
Technical Drawing-Mastering an Exact Likeness** *(Drawing II)*

DRAWING THE EYES

It is particularly important to draw the right eye while at the same time the left eye is drawn.

Close up of the left eye continued.

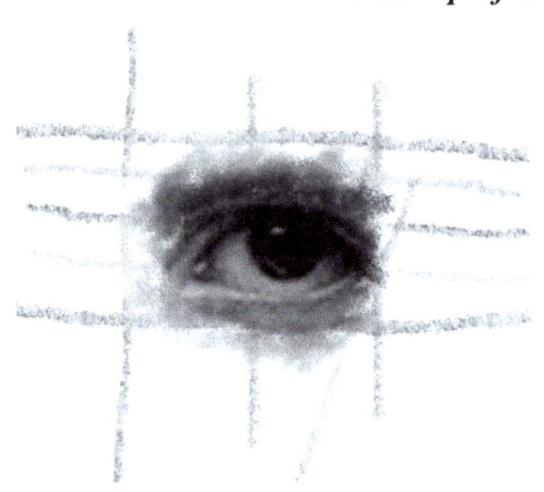

Tone the remainder of the lower eyelid. This will complete this part for now.

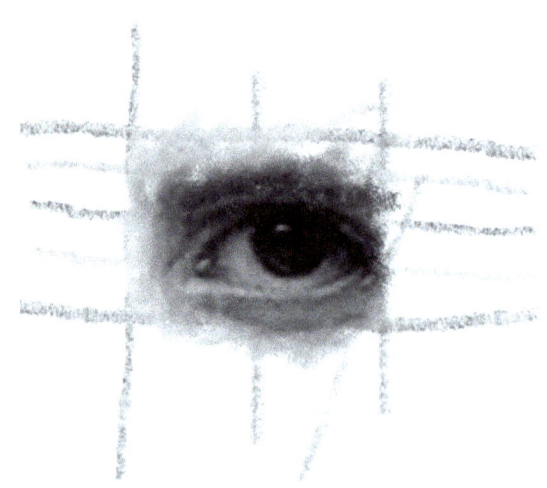

To add some shadow, blend the material into the bridge of the nose.

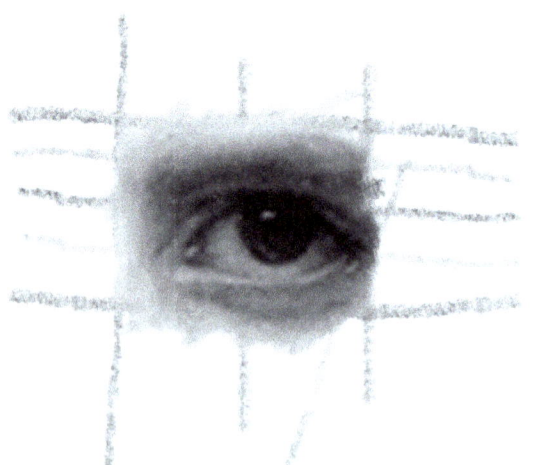

Use the horizontal and vertical lines as smoothing material and smooth the upper brow and the bridge of the nose.

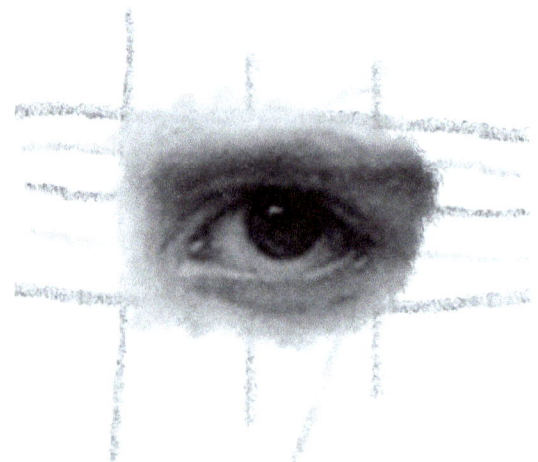

Add more material to the upper brow blending and smoothing the area around the eye. For now, the eye is finished.

You Can Draw Portraits:
Technical Drawing-Mastering an Exact Likeness

(Drawing II)

COMPLETION OF THE EYES

Once the map is set with the vertical, horizontal, and diagonal lines you will see how easy it is to draw the eyes. Blend in the eyes using the map lines that have already been placed. For working material add more charcoal in between the eyes. Wait for the detail stage to complete the eyes. By drawing the eyes simultaneously, the portrait's progress should look like the following illustrations. In this distant view of the canvas, observe how the eye's placement comes together.

The eye process as viewed from left to right top to bottom.

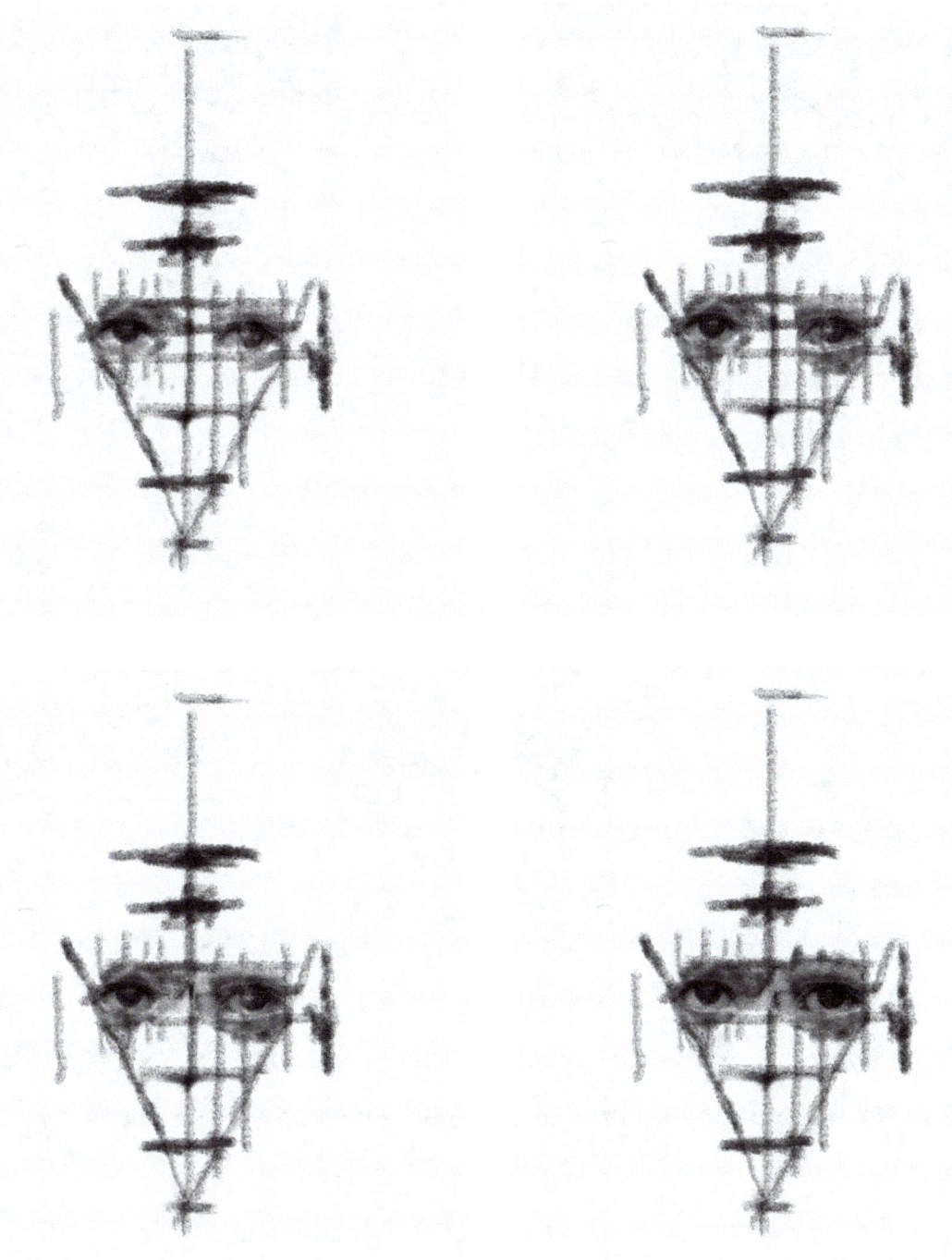

You Can Draw Portraits:
Technical Drawing-Mastering an Exact Likeness *(Drawing II)*

The eye process as viewed from left to right top to bottom.
Continued

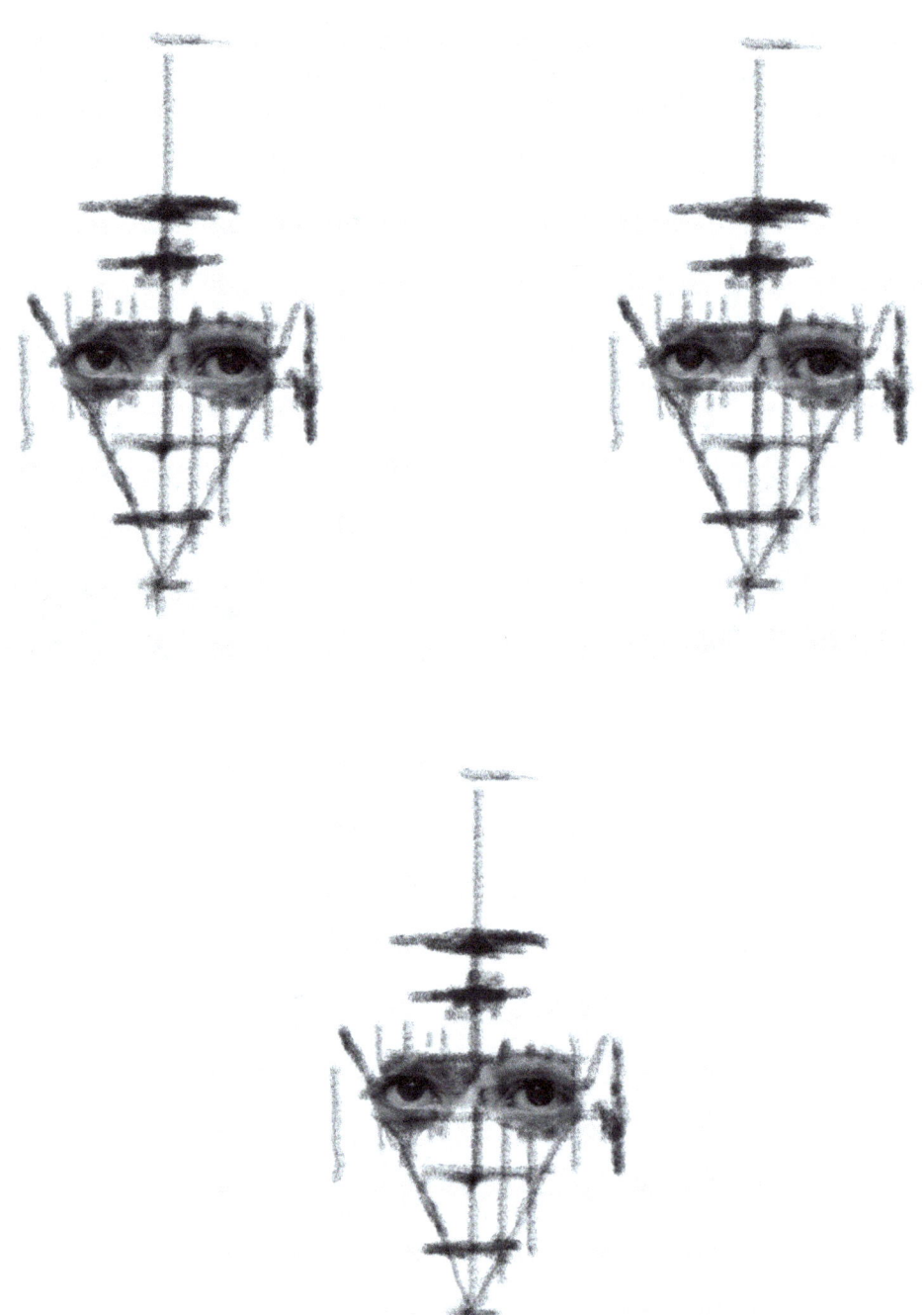

For more information on how to draw the eye and for a free tutorial check out my website at:

http://www.davidrite.com

DRAWING III:
Section: 5

"Don't aim for success if you want it; just do what you love and believe in, and it will come naturally."

~ David Frost

DRAWING III

FINDING MAP POINTS FOR THE LIPS / EARS / NOSE

The focus in this section is on the lips, ears, and nose. To find the placement of the lips, ears, and nose use the same method explained in the previous section *(continue to divide the map lines into halves)*. Drawing the nose will give an exact and accurate location for drawing the lips. Furthermore, dividing up the horizontal and vertical map lines will make it easier to find the placement for the ears.

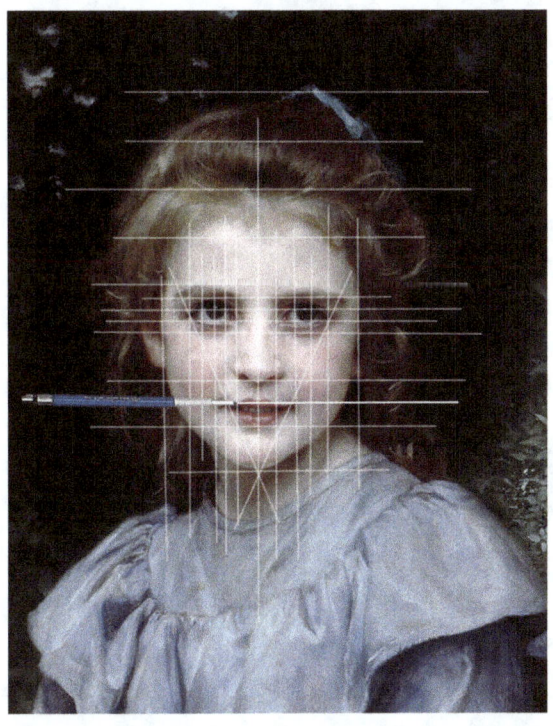

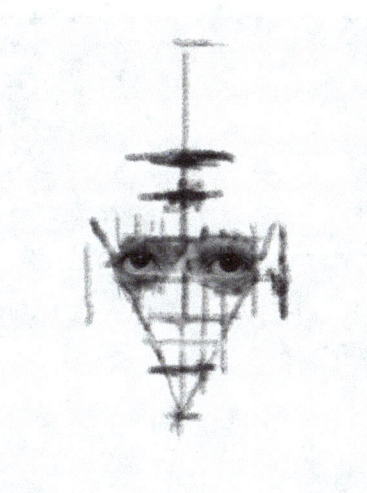

The upper lip's location is found by dividing the tip of the nose and the bottom of the lips' horizontal limit lines in half.

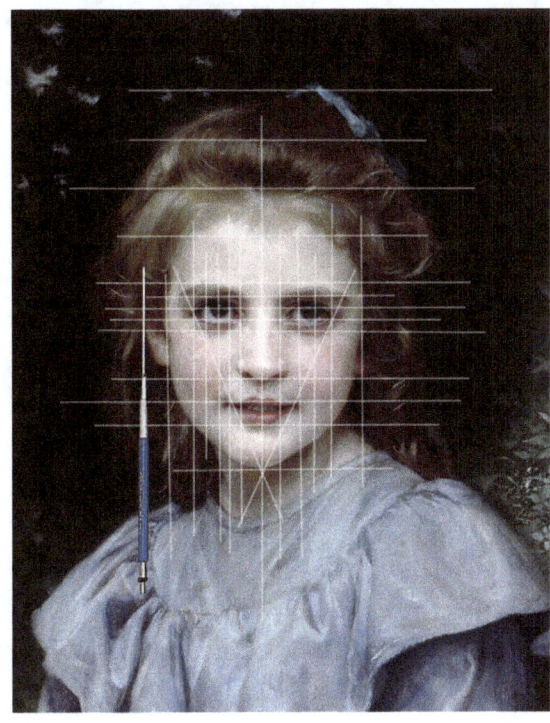

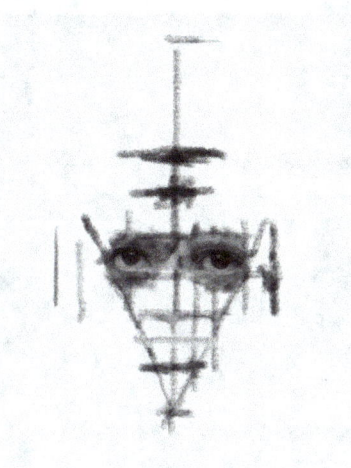

The right ear's outside location is measured from the corner of the right eye's vertical line to the right vertical cheek line, go that same distance outward from the cheek line and place a mark.

You Can Draw Portraits:
Technical Drawing-Mastering an Exact Likeness *(Drawing III)*

The horizontal, vertical, and diagonal lines have been used as identifying placement positions as well as for smoothing and blending. Now in combination with the remainder of the road map lines we will now be moving onto the next phase, the nose. We have added some charcoal for shaping the nose. In the illustrations below we will start to draw the nose.

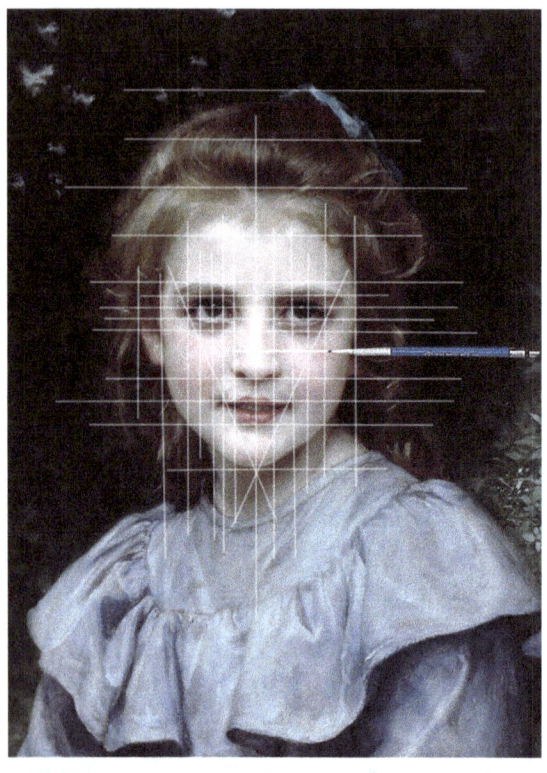

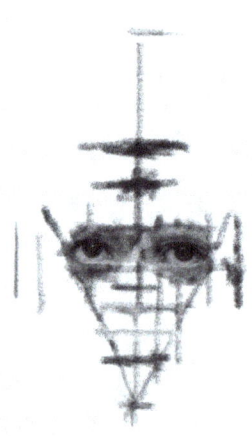

Place a mark in the middle of the nose which will aid in completing the nose. It is halfway between the lower eyelid and the tip of the nose.

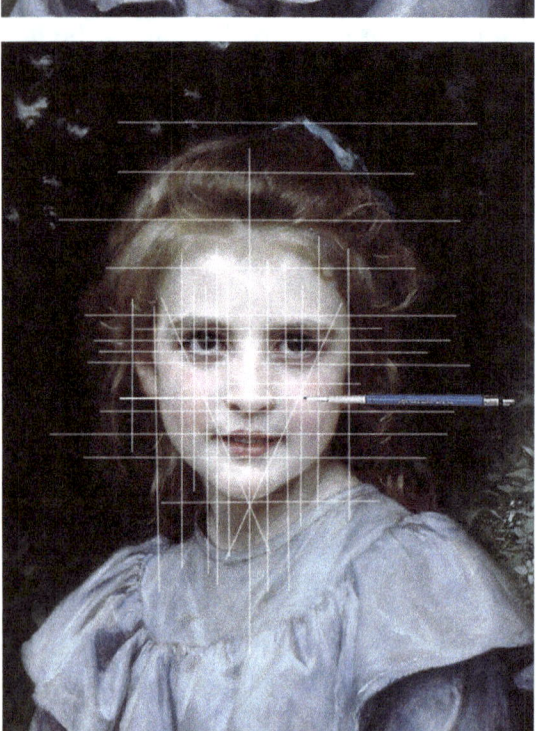

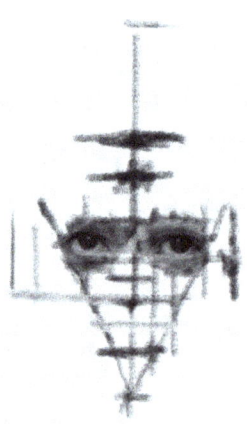

By placing a horizontal mark, it will visually show where the bottom of the ear is placed. This locates the midpoint of the nostrils and how to find it in relation to the ear.

You Can Draw Portraits:
Technical Drawing-Mastering an Exact Likeness *(Drawing III)*

DRAWING THE NOSE AND THE MOUTH

The images below are a look at the nose and mouth process from a distance.

View the following illustrations from left to right and top to bottom.

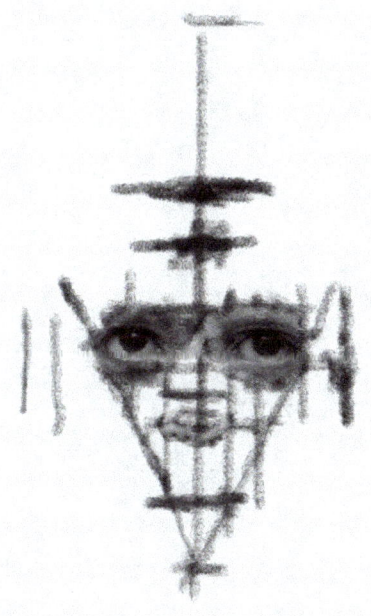

Begin the nose by drawing the tip at this horizontal mark.

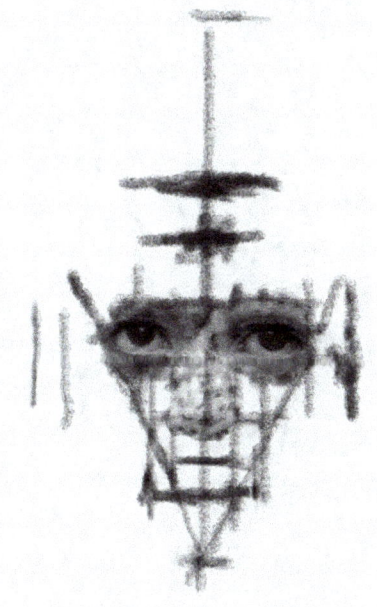

Continue to add and blend in the charcoal while toning the sides of the nose.

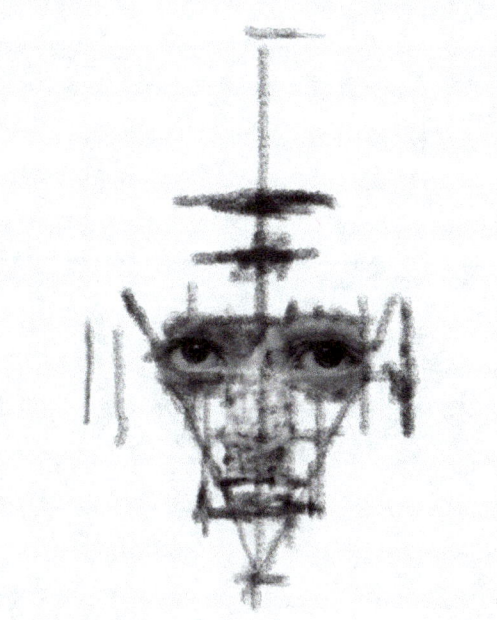

Start the upper lip and mark the bottom lip.

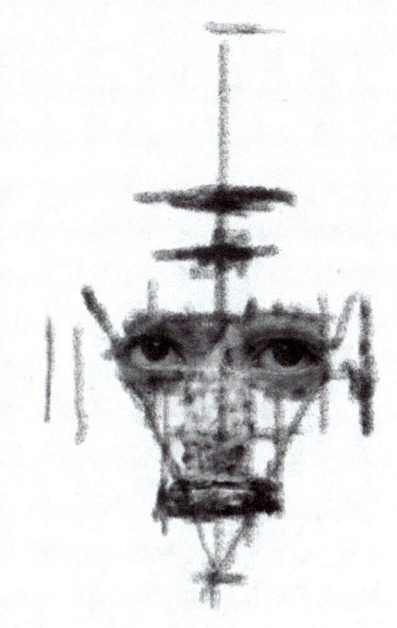

Add charcoal around the mouth to use for blending and shaping the lips.

**You Can Draw Portraits:
Technical Drawing-Mastering an Exact Likeness** *(Drawing III)*

DRAWING THE NOSE AND THE MOUTH

A look at the nose and mouth process from a distance. *(Continued)*

View the following illustrations from left to right and top to bottom.

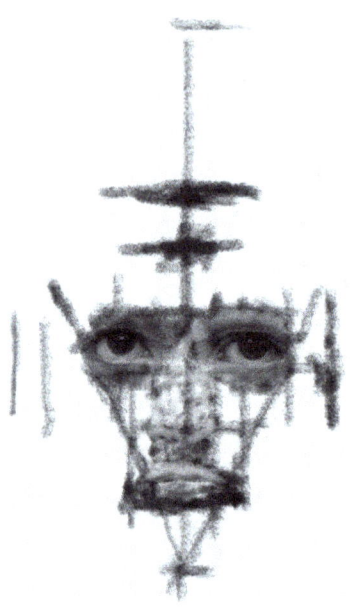

Follow the horizontal and vertical lines that mark the ends of the mouth.

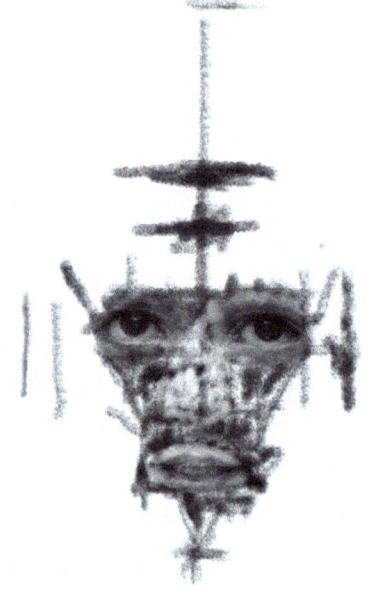

Just block in the cheek area with material and save the detail for later.

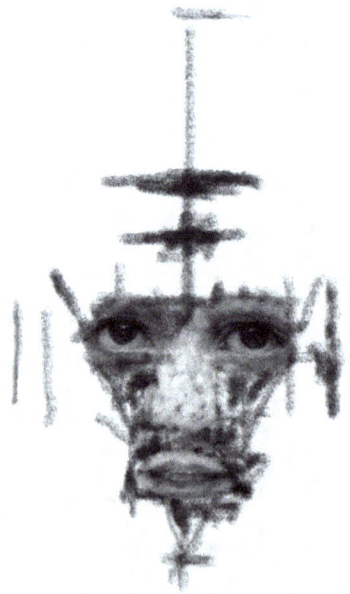

Use the vertical and horizontal lines as material to blend and smooth out the charcoal to give the nose some depth.

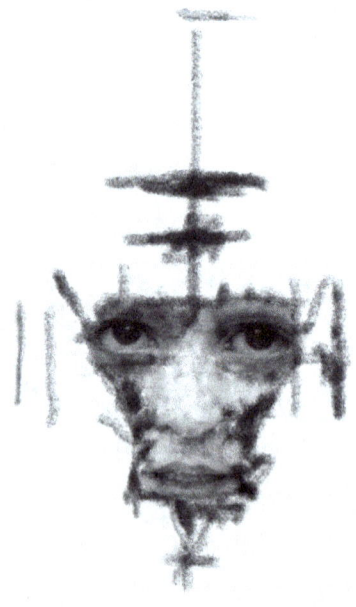

Now subtract and blend the material to tone and shape the mouth. The nose and mouth are now starting to look real.

You Can Draw Portraits:
Technical Drawing-Mastering an Exact Likeness *(Drawing III)*

DRAWING THE NOSE AND THE MOUTH

A look at the nose and mouth process from a distance. *(Continued)*

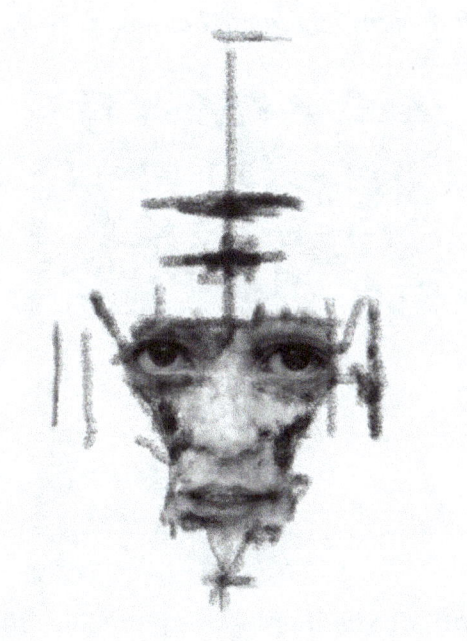

After smoothing out the cheek area then proceed to start with the outer shape of the face.

NOTE: As viewed from far away these steps may seem a little confusing. So, in the next few pages, I will demonstrate these steps we just completed in a close-up view.

"Tis a lesson you should heed:
Try, try, try again.
If at first you don't succeed,
Try, try, try again."

~ William Edward Hickson

**You Can Draw Portraits:
Technical Drawing-Mastering an Exact Likeness** *(Drawing III)*

DRAWING THE NOSE

The illustrations below are close-up views of each of the steps taken previously while drawing the nose and lips. The vertical and horizontal lines tell us where to draw each portion of the nose and lips. The following is focusing just on the nose. When the nose has been established, then the lips will follow.

View the following illustrations from left to right and top to bottom.

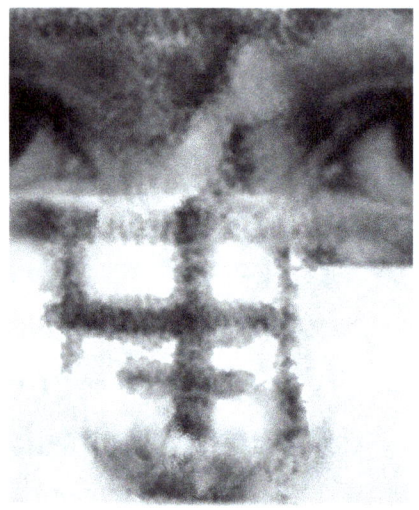

In this closeup notice that the nose divides on the vertical axis.

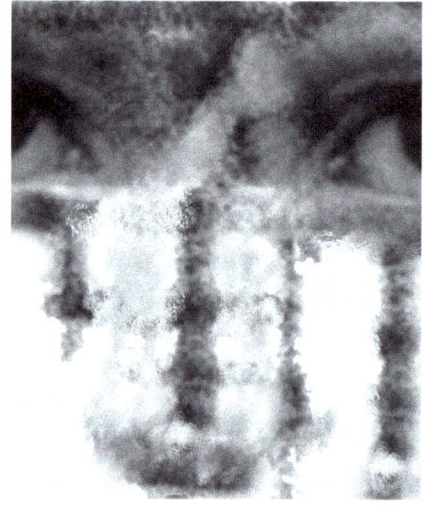

Continue shading by using the lines that crossed the nose as material to obtain the right tonal value of the nose.

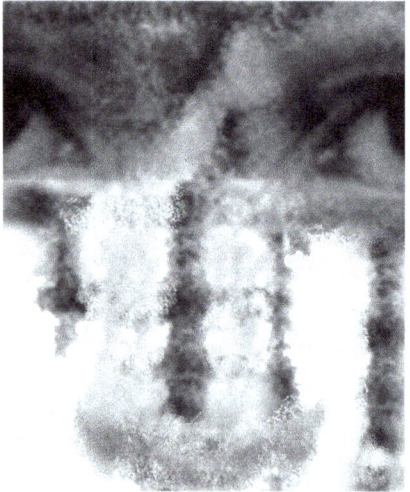

Notice that the right nostril with the vertical line is matching the inside of the right eye. Continue to shade and blend the nose.

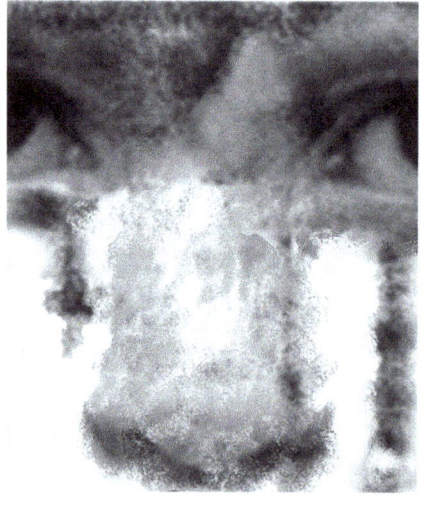

Use the vertical axis line as shading material. Notice the vertical line coming down from the inside left eye showing the left side of the nose.

You Can Draw Portraits:
Technical Drawing-Mastering an Exact Likeness *(Drawing III)*

Below are closeup views of each of the steps taken previously while drawing the nose. Use each of the vertical and horizontal lines to locate where to draw each portion of the nose.

View the following illustrations from left to right and top to bottom.

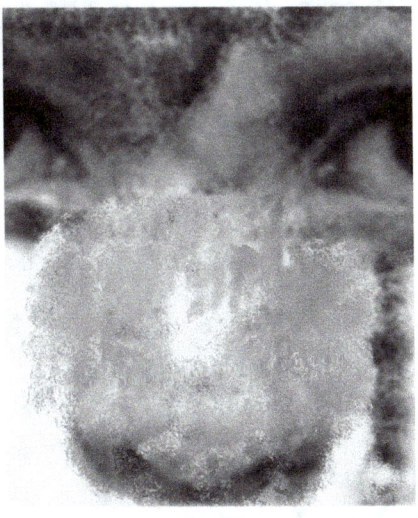

Restate the bottom of the nose by adding more material to the nostrils. Begin to shade the cheeks connecting them with the nose.

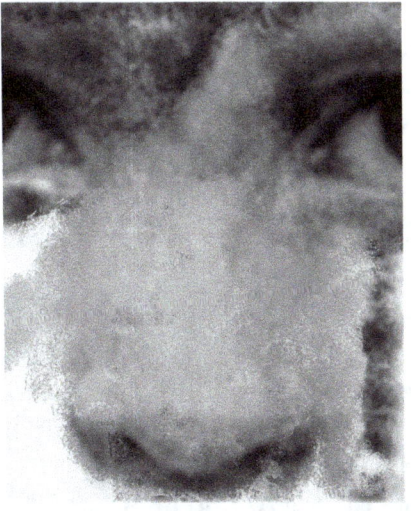

Make tonal shifts from the bridge of the nose and its sides to give depth to the nose. Then shade the front of the nose and its tip.

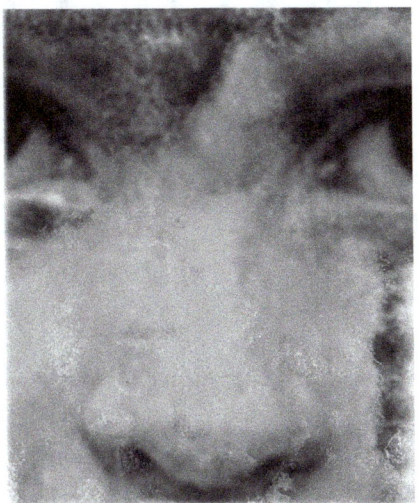

The nose has found its proper position in the facial features of the model. Now it is time to move onto the mouth and lips.

NOTE: We have completed the nose for now. The final completion of the nose will be done in Section 7.

**You Can Draw Portraits:
Technical Drawing-Mastering an Exact Likeness** *(Drawing III)*

DRAWING THE MOUTH

View the following illustrations from left to right and top to bottom.

Here in the following illustrations are closeup views of each of the steps taken previously while drawing the lips. Using each of the vertical, diagonal, and horizontal lines will show where to draw the lips.

In the following illustrations of the mouth, I wanted to demonstrate the importance of all of the mapping lines. Notice that the lines shown in the images are figuratively demonstrated as what the artist sees when drawing the mouth. Having almost completed the eyes they still can be used for lining up other features such as the mouth.

Notice how each end of the mouth lines up with the vertical lines corresponding with the eyes' iris. The horizontal lines that have been divided in halves now show where the lips will be drawn.

Dividing the horizontal lines in half will enable us to see the top of the lower lip. Divide the vertical lines in half to find the tips of the upper lip.

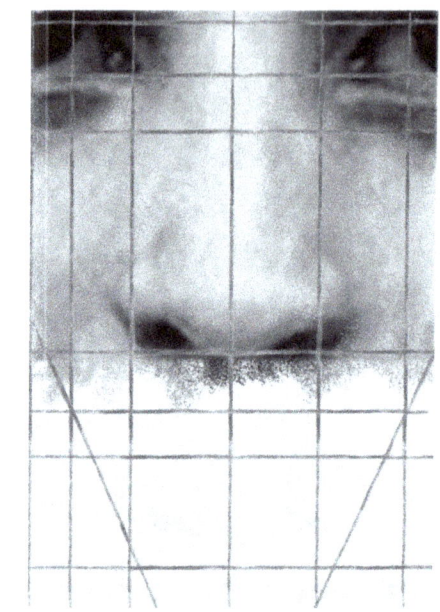

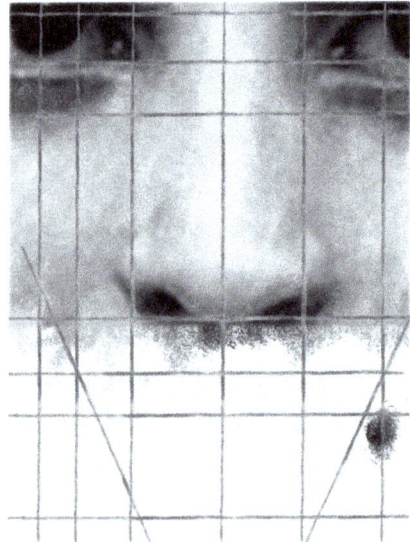

The vertical line that corresponds with the inside of the left iris shows where the left side of the mouth should be marked.

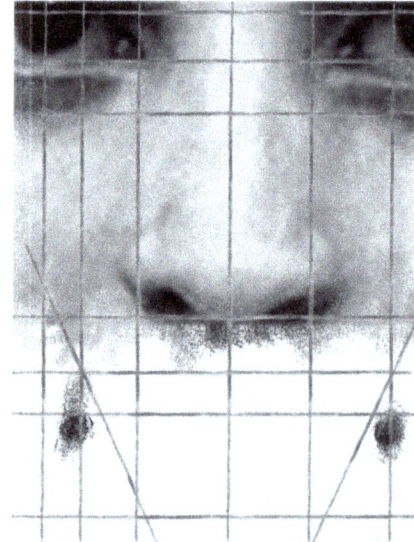

By holding the pencil vertically, notice that the right side of the mouth lines directly under the inside of the right eye's iris.

NOTE: The lines seen in each picture represent imaginary lines seen by the artist as he or she transfers those lines as marks onto the canvas for mapping the facial features. Any slight variations that exist between points can easily be found by dividing the lines in half and marking them.

**You Can Draw Portraits:
Technical Drawing-Mastering an Exact Likeness** *(Drawing III)*

View the following illustrations from left to right and top to bottom.

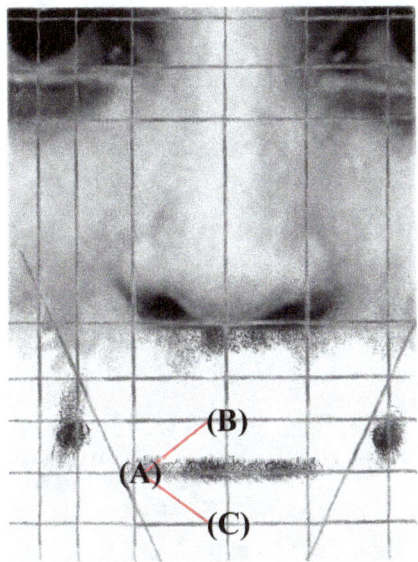

To find the middle of the lips just add another horizontal line *(A)* by dividing the two existing lines *(B&C)* in half. Now mark the middle of the mouth.

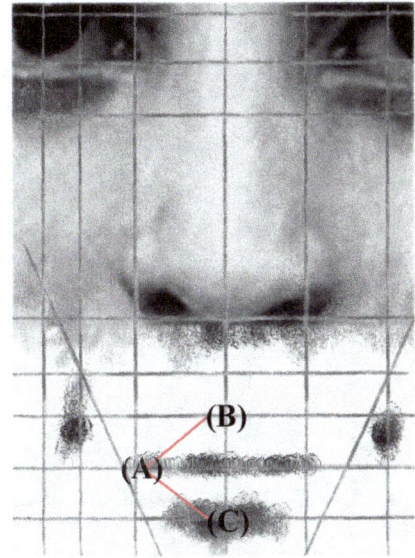

Then shade line *(C)* to mark where the end of the upper part of the bottom lip begins.

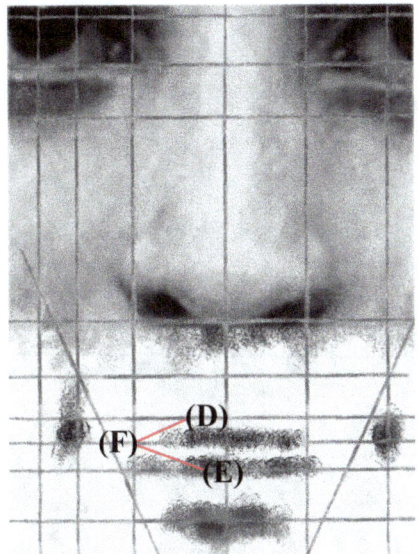

Divide the horizontal lines *(D&E)* to find the bottom of the upper lip *(F)*. Then mark it by shading along the line.

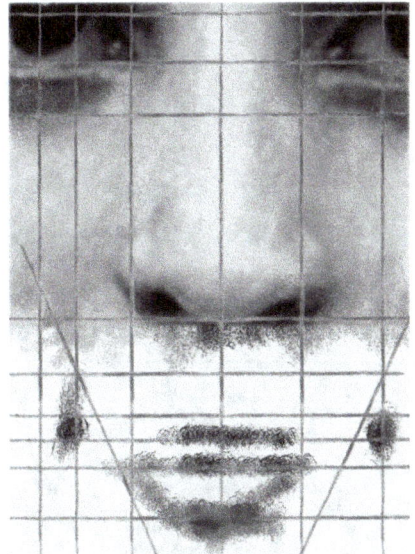

Having identified the vertical lines running on either side of the nose then shade the lower lip by adding more charcoal and blending it.

NOTE: When there is still a variation in finding a point, divide the lines into halves and continue this method and eventually the point will fall into place.

You Can Draw Portraits:
Technical Drawing-Mastering an Exact Likeness *(Drawing III)*

View the following illustrations from left to right and top to bottom.

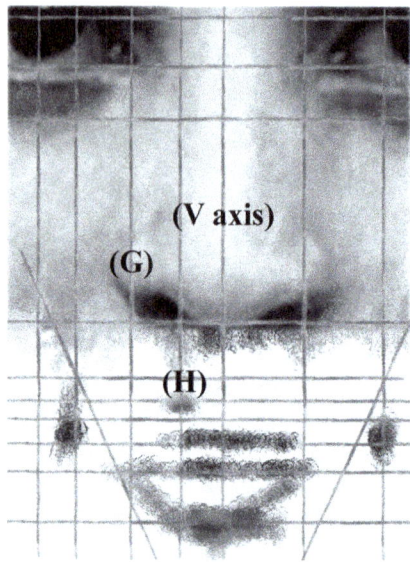

Divide the vertical axis *(V axis)* and the vertical line *(G)* on the right side of the nose in half in order to find the upper point of the lip *(H)*.

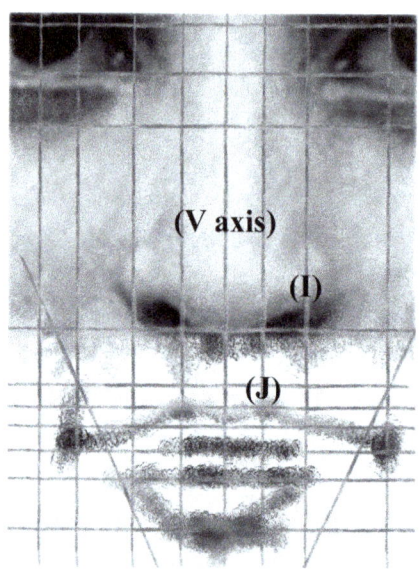

To find the left upper point *(J)* of the upper lip, just divide the vertical axis *(V axis)* and the outer vertical line *(I)*, of the left side of the nose in half.

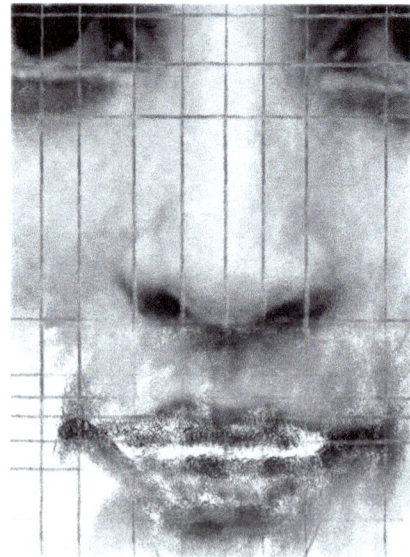

Since identifying the mouth's basic shape, it is time to shade in the lower and upper lips. Also, at this point go ahead and start shading in under the nose and lower lips.

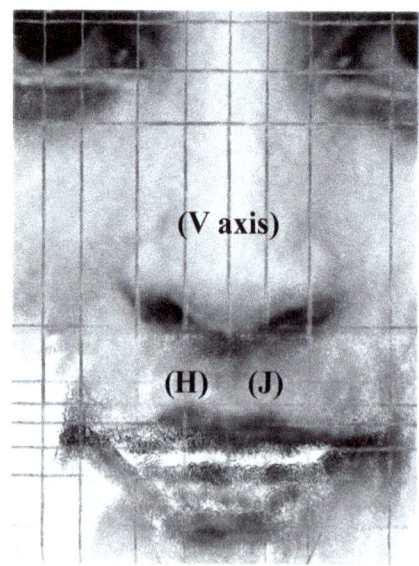

Continue to shade in the left side of the upper lip *(J)* and restate the lip's right-side apex *(H)*.

You Can Draw Portraits:
Technical Drawing-Mastering an Exact Likeness *(Drawing III)*

View the following illustrations from left to right and top to bottom.

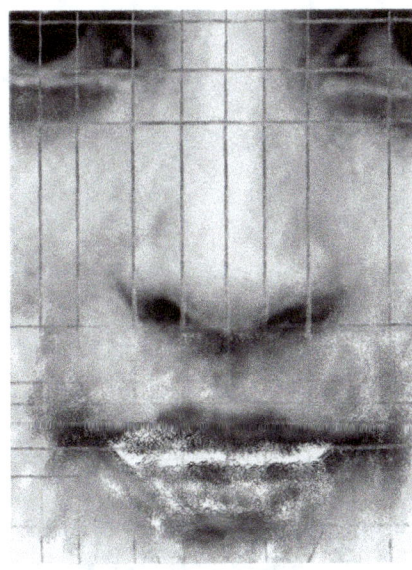

Shade in more of the lower lip and the right side of the cheek, then add more material for the next step.

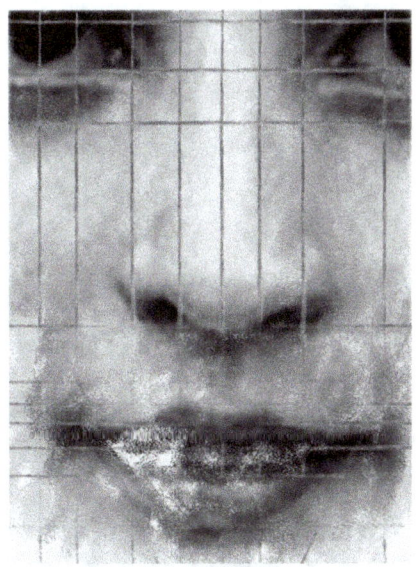

Continue to shade in the upper lip's left side and start to hint at the teeth. Now the mouth is starting to really take shape.

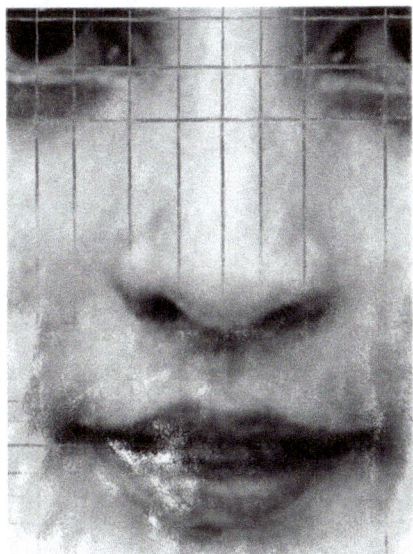

Having already found the lower lip's upper portion, now darken it in. Follow up with a light tone to give the mouth some depth. Next, lightly shade in the lower lip by continuing to hint at the teeth.

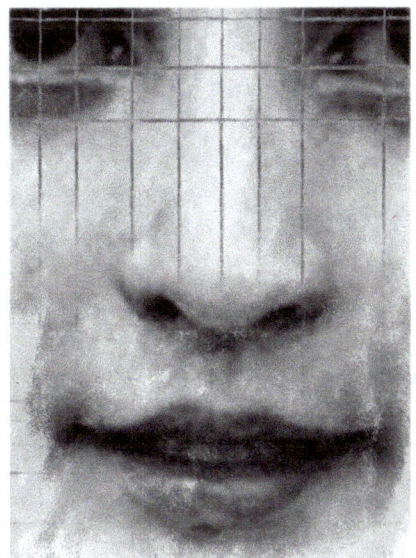

Shade the lower lip and the right side of the mouth. To obtain the correct tones follow the same procedure as before with the left side of the lips.

You Can Draw Portraits:
Technical Drawing-Mastering an Exact Likeness *(Drawing III)*

View the following illustrations from left to right and top to bottom.

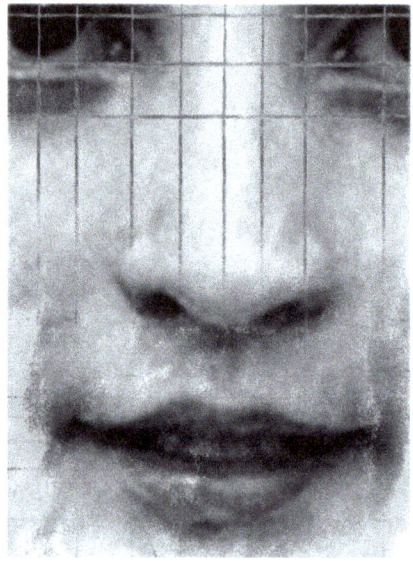 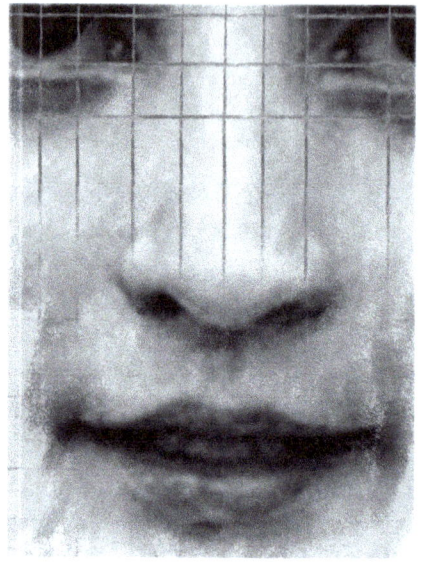

Use the horizontal and vertical lines as material for shading and continue to fill in the cheeks.

Continue to blend the cheeks, under the nose, and lips using the vertical and horizontal lines as shading material.

"Art enables us to find ourselves and lose ourselves at the same time."

~ Thomas Merton

**You Can Draw Portraits:
Technical Drawing-Mastering an Exact Likeness** *(Drawing III)*

It is easier to see the contrast between the lips and teeth after accenting the nose and lips. However, it is especially important to wait until the final stages to finish the highlights of the nose and lips. This part of the portrait is finished for now.

The detail stage is for polishing and highlighting the portrait.

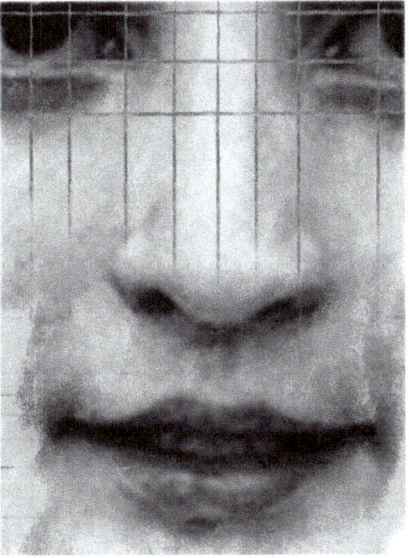

The next section is on establishing the jaw and cheek lines.

You are doing GREAT!

You have now successfully completed the eyes, nose, and the mouth stages!

(See Section 7, Drawing V: Stages for Detailing / Highlighting)

DRAWING IV:
Section: 6

"That which we persist in doing becomes easier to do, not that the nature of the thing has changed but that our power to do has increased."

~ Ralph Waldo Emerson

DRAWING IV

ESTABLISHING CHIN AND CHEEK LINES

Diagonal measurements are used in conjunction with the horizontal and vertical lines to find angles that are then transferred to the work. To find the outer shape of the face continue to divide each horizontal and vertical lines in half until the horizontal and vertical lines reach the location that matches the diagonal reference point *(as seen below)*.

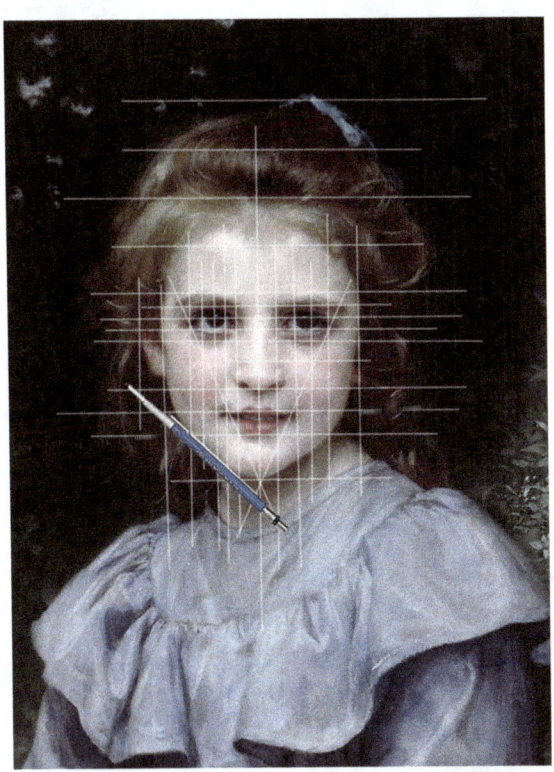

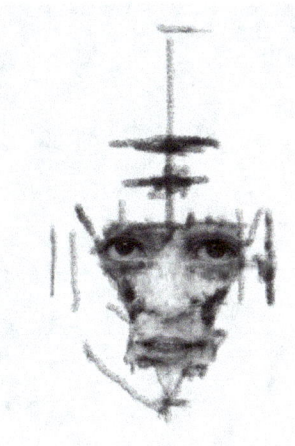

It is time to find the width of the lower right jaw. Use the vertical axis to draw a diagonal line up from the chin to the outer vertical right cheek. This marks the chin line.

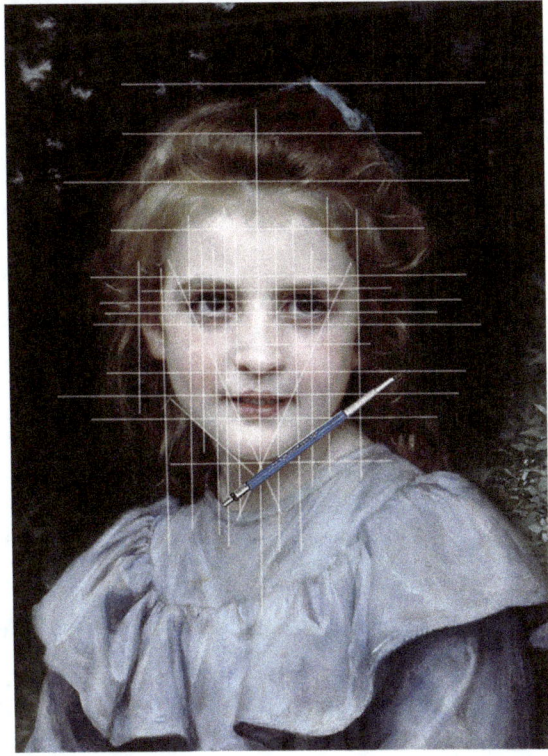

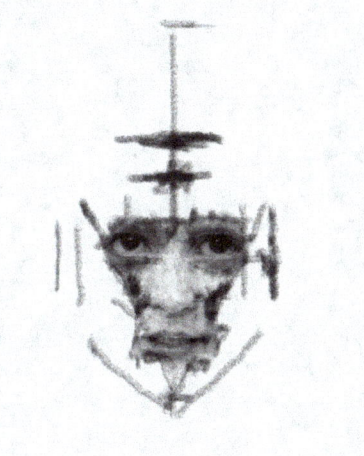

Using the same directions as above *(right side jaw)*, duplicate that on the left side to find her left jaw line.

**You Can Draw Portraits:
Technical Drawing-Mastering an Exact Likeness** *(Drawing IV)*

COMPLETING THE CHIN AND CHEEK LINES

This part continues to mark the diagonal lines for the outer cheeks and adding extra charcoal as a base for toning material to be used later for blending *(see below)*.

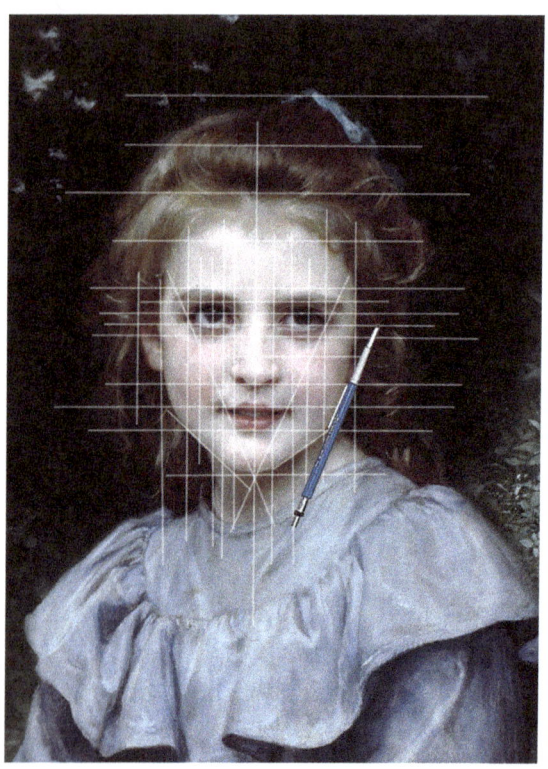

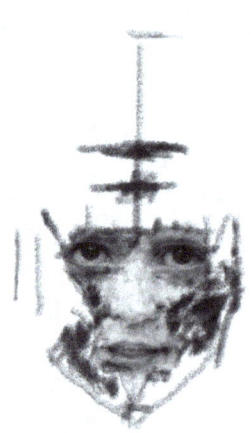

The diagonal placement of the jaw is found by using the horizontal line at the bottom of the mouth up to the horizontal line at the tip of the nose. Then draw a line and add some material to be used for blending later.

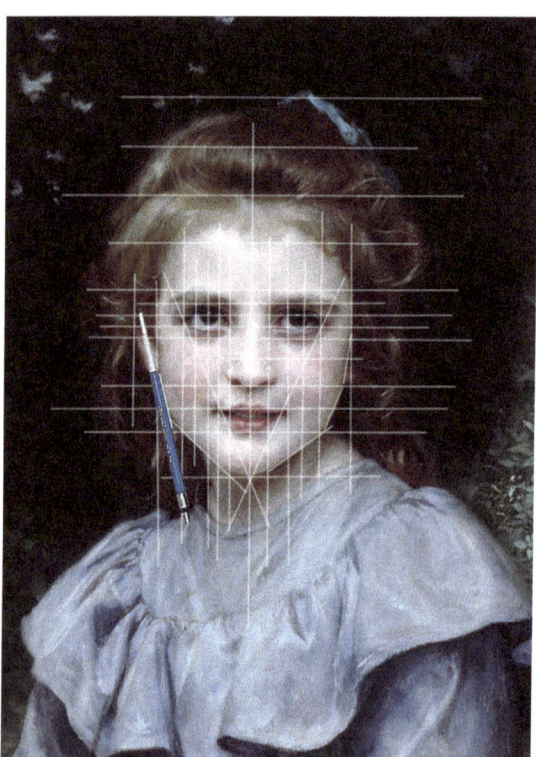

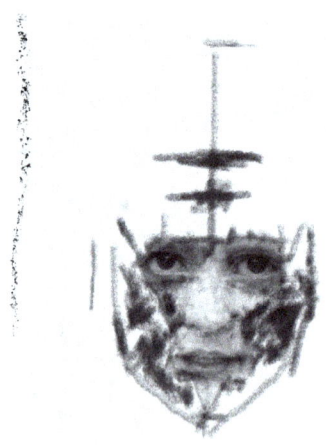

Use the same directions as above to mark her right jaw. Then on both sides draw a vertical line from the horizontal line at the tip of the nose up to the horizontal brow line to complete the cheek outline.

You Can Draw Portraits:
Technical Drawing-Mastering an Exact Likeness   *(Drawing IV)*

BEGINNING THE FOREHEAD LINES

Charcoal is added as toning material to be used for blending and creating the values needed for the face. Keep in mind that the same steps are used for the right side that are used for the left side. This aids in keeping the drawing uniform and the placements accurate.

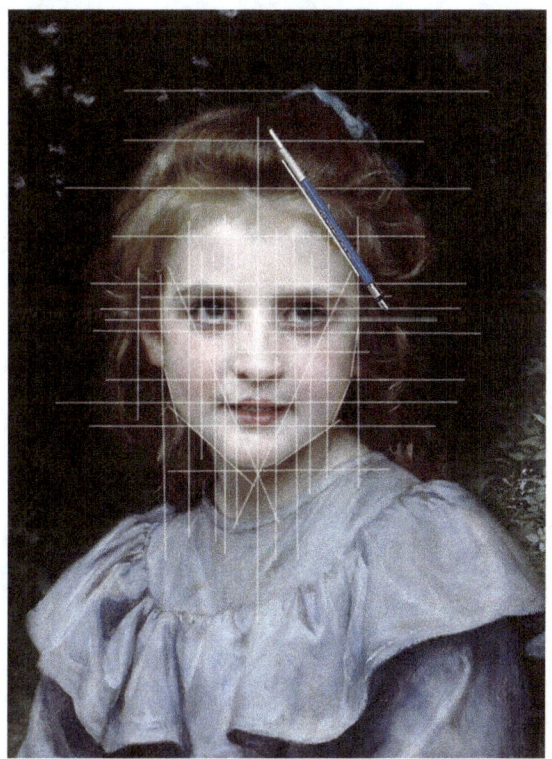

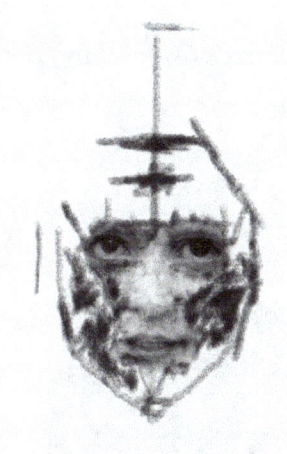

Mark the point where the diagonal line meets the vertical cheek line *(temple area)* up to the horizontal hairline on the left side of the forehead. This is the angle that completes the left side of the facial outline.

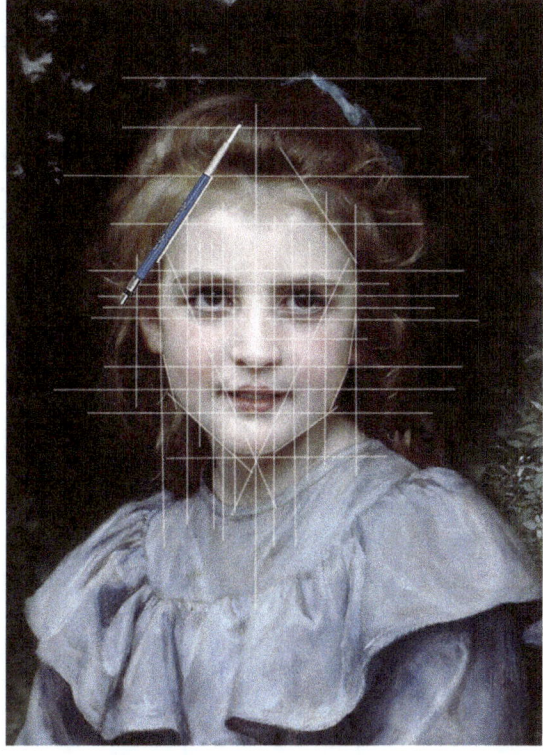

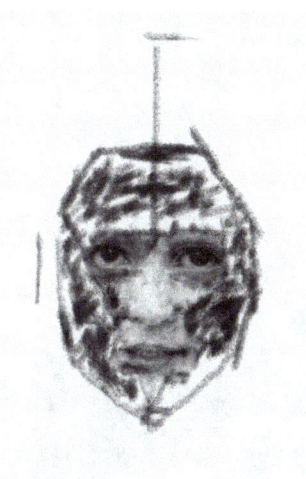

Use the same directions as above to mark her right brow and forehead. This completes the facial outline. Then add some charcoal to be used for the shading.

73

You Can Draw Portraits:
Technical Drawing-Mastering an Exact Likeness   *(Drawing IV)*

SMOOTHING THE FACE

Pay close attention to the tonal variations of the subject. The tones that are transferred to the drawing will aid in achieving the depth to the facial features that are needed to attain the exact likeness. The following illustrations show in five stages the toning of the face using a stump, fingers, and a kneaded eraser.

Illustrations of smoothing the face, they are to be viewed left to right and top to bottom.

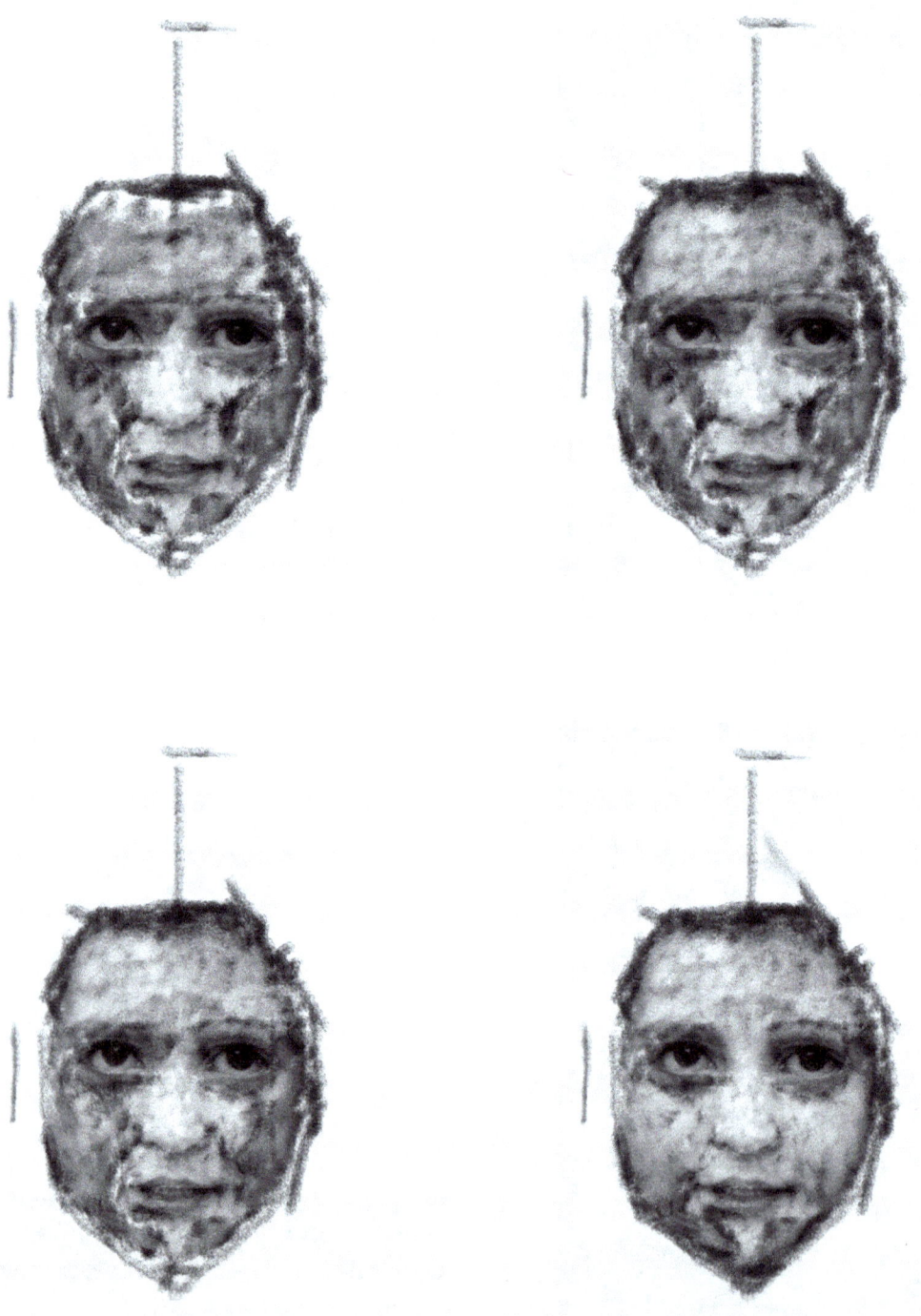

**You Can Draw Portraits:
Technical Drawing-Mastering an Exact Likeness** *(Drawing IV)*

SMOOTHING THE FACE

Continue to pay close attention to the tonal variations, which gives exactness to the facial features.

Illustrations of smoothing the face. Continued

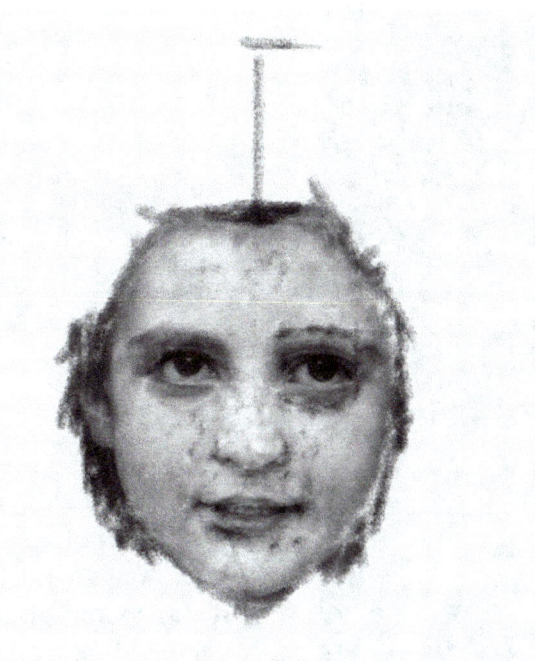

TIP: Using your fingers as a tool for smudging can be very useful in obtaining the right tonal values.

NOTE: The remainder of the detail and highlighting of the drawing can be viewed in the following section.

As for now it is time to work on the Hair and Neck.

You Can Draw Portraits:
Technical Drawing-Mastering an Exact Likeness *(Drawing IV)*

BEGINNING THE HAIR AND NECK

While looking at the model as a reference, follow these instructions in order to find the limit lines for the hair. The limit line for the right side of the hair is found by measuring out the same distance width from the vertical cheek line to the vertical line of the ear. Place a vertical mark from the horizontal line at the tip of the nose up to the horizontal forehead line.

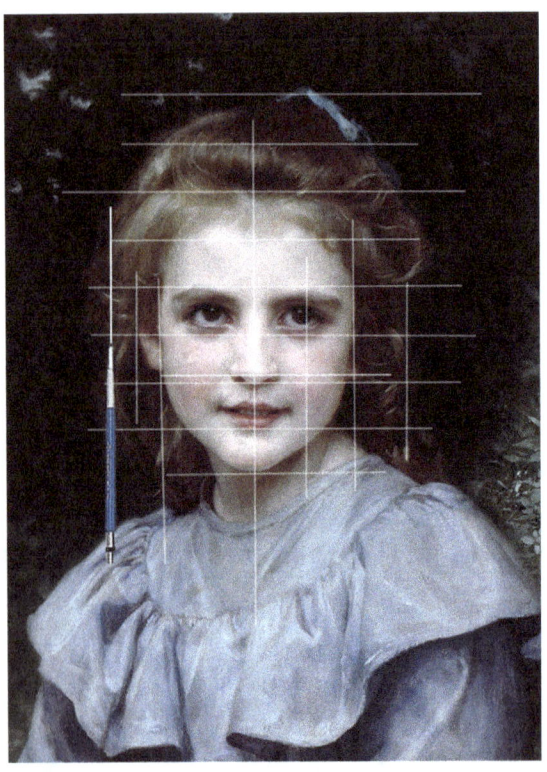

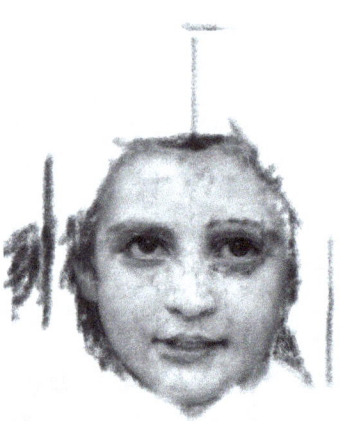

For the left side, measure the same distance width from the vertical brow line to the cheek line, then go out from the cheek line, the same distance and place a marker. Next draw a vertical line from the horizontal chin line up to the brow line.

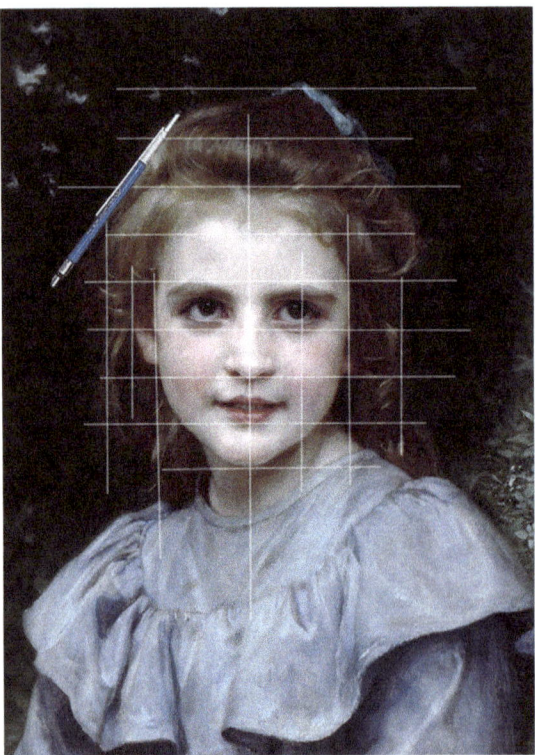

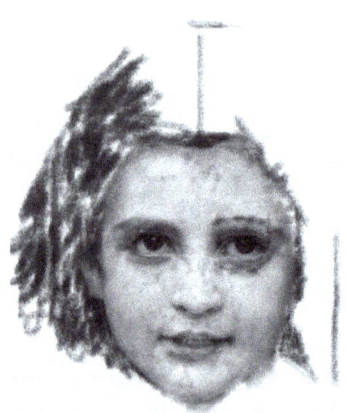

The top right side is found from the top of the last hair limit line to the halfway point between the top of the hair and the top of the head. Draw a diagonal line up to that halfway point.

You Can Draw Portraits:
Technical Drawing-Mastering an Exact Likeness   *(Drawing IV)*

It is important while drawing the hair to remember that each hair strand is not seen. When looking at a person from a distance only a representation *(or whole)* of the hair is seen. A mistake frequently made in drawing a subject's hair is to try and draw every strand of hair. It is easy to get lost in striving to make every stroke of the drawing medium represent each hair. This overworks the image and does not have a natural effect. Be sure to look at the hair as a block or a mass that can later be detailed.

In these steps adding some charcoal material to use for toning and blending will aid in obtaining the correct tonal values. In addition, using the material from the vertical, horizontal, and diagonal lines as blending material will help in transforming the image into a more complete depiction.

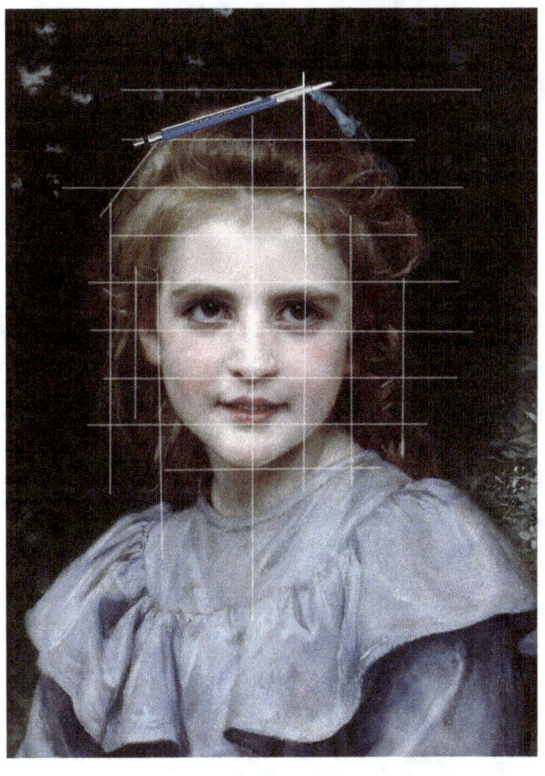

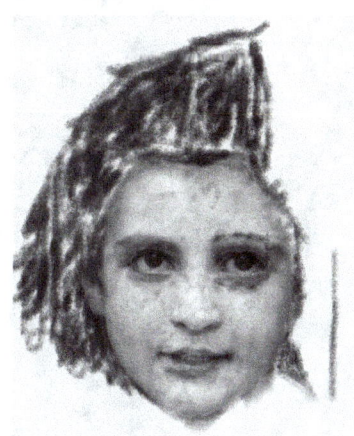

To locate the top of the hair, use the horizontal head limit line up to the top of the hair line and draw a diagonal line. Then add more material.

"By an inch it's a cinch, by a yard it's hard."

~ Stephen Lee

You Can Draw Portraits:
Technical Drawing-Mastering an Exact Likeness *(Drawing IV)*

During this process, it is important to use the charcoal left by any of the previous vertical, horizontal, and diagonal lines as blending material. The extra material that is already on the support will serve to smooth out the image. Do not erase the lines to just add more charcoal. This will save time and materials. Continue using the same formula we have used up to this point *(which is dividing the lines in half to find the mapping points)*.

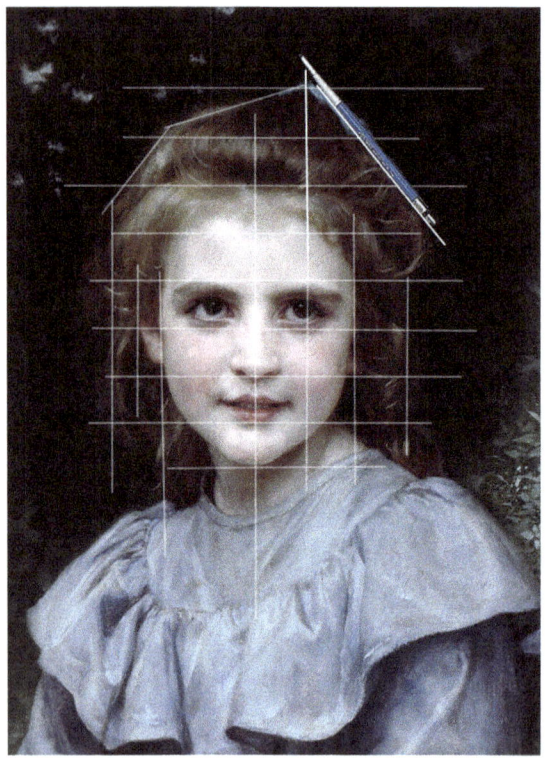

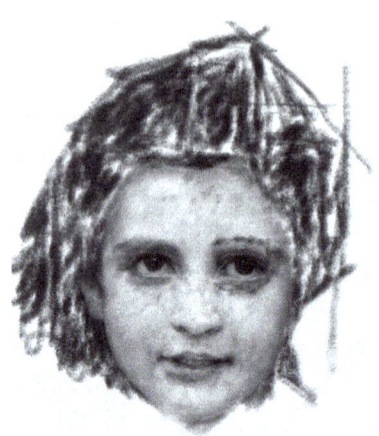

The top left side of the hair is found by following the vertical line from the left iris up to the top of the hair limit line. Then draw a diagonal line, down from that point, past the hair limit line on the left. This completes the mapping of the hair.

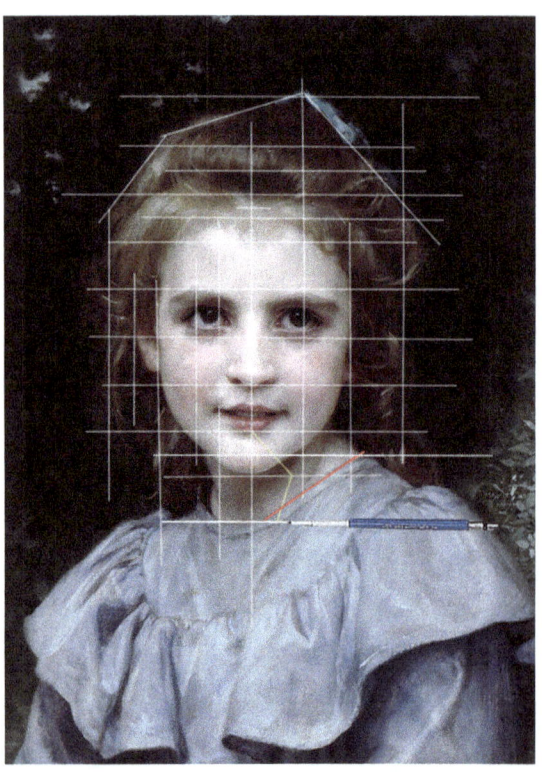

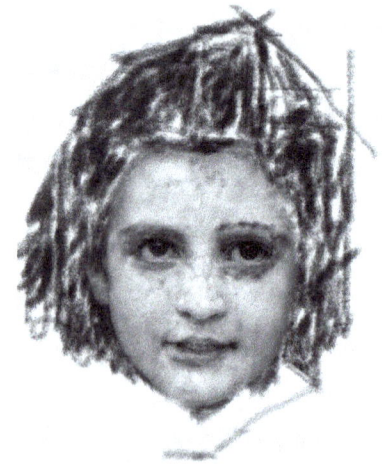

The neck line is found by going down the same distance from the bottom of the mouth to the bottom of the chin. Draw a limit line. Now draw a diagonal line up from that point to the halfway point between the mouth and the chin.

**You Can Draw Portraits:
Technical Drawing-Mastering an Exact Likeness** *(Drawing IV)*

Once these limit lines are found, add some charcoal to aid in blending the tonal values for the hair and neck. Now that the material and guides are in place it is time to move onto the next section that will show the steps of adding material, blending, smoothing, and erasing in order to complete the portrait.

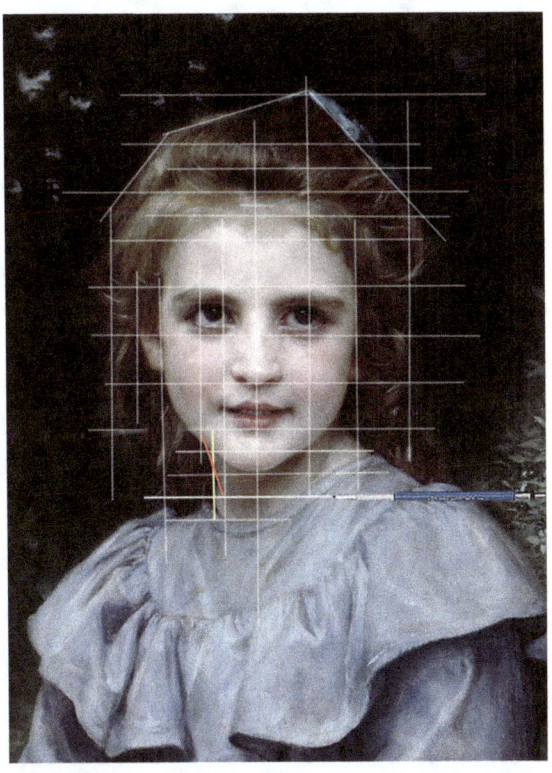

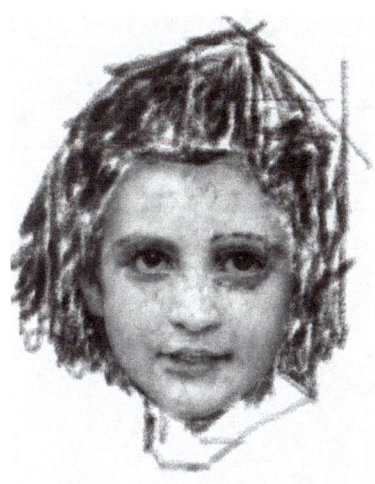

For the right side of the neck, divide the vertical eye lines in half. Draw a line down from the horizontal halfway line of the chin and mouth down to the halfway chin and neckline. Now angle diagonally at that point to the neck limit line.

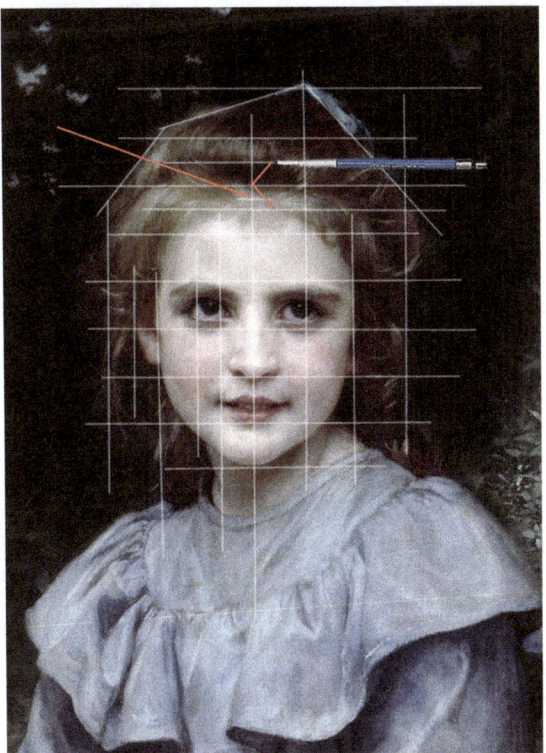

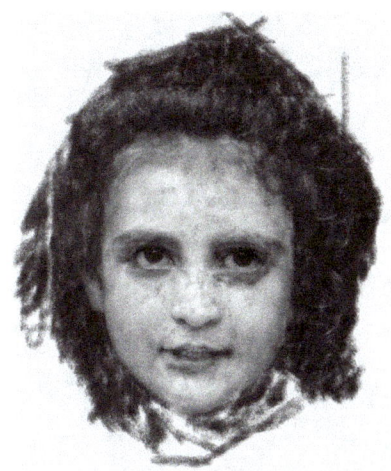

The red lines are added to show the division in the hairline. Divide the hairline and the forehead line in half, this is the start of the bangs, and the highlights of the hair. Use the kneaded eraser to start making the lighter tones in the upper wave of the model's hair.

DRAWING V:
Section: 7

*"Success is simply this;
Doing what's RITE, the RITE way, at the
RITE time, every time."*

~David Rite

DRAWING V

**STAGES FOR DRAWING THE PORTRAIT:
FINISHING THE HAIR AND NECK**

The following images are a quick look at the ending stages of the hair and neck. It also covers detailing and finishing of the portrait. The view is at a distance to get an overall visual. These illustrations will show the addition and subtraction of the charcoal material in order to obtain the desired look for the portrait.

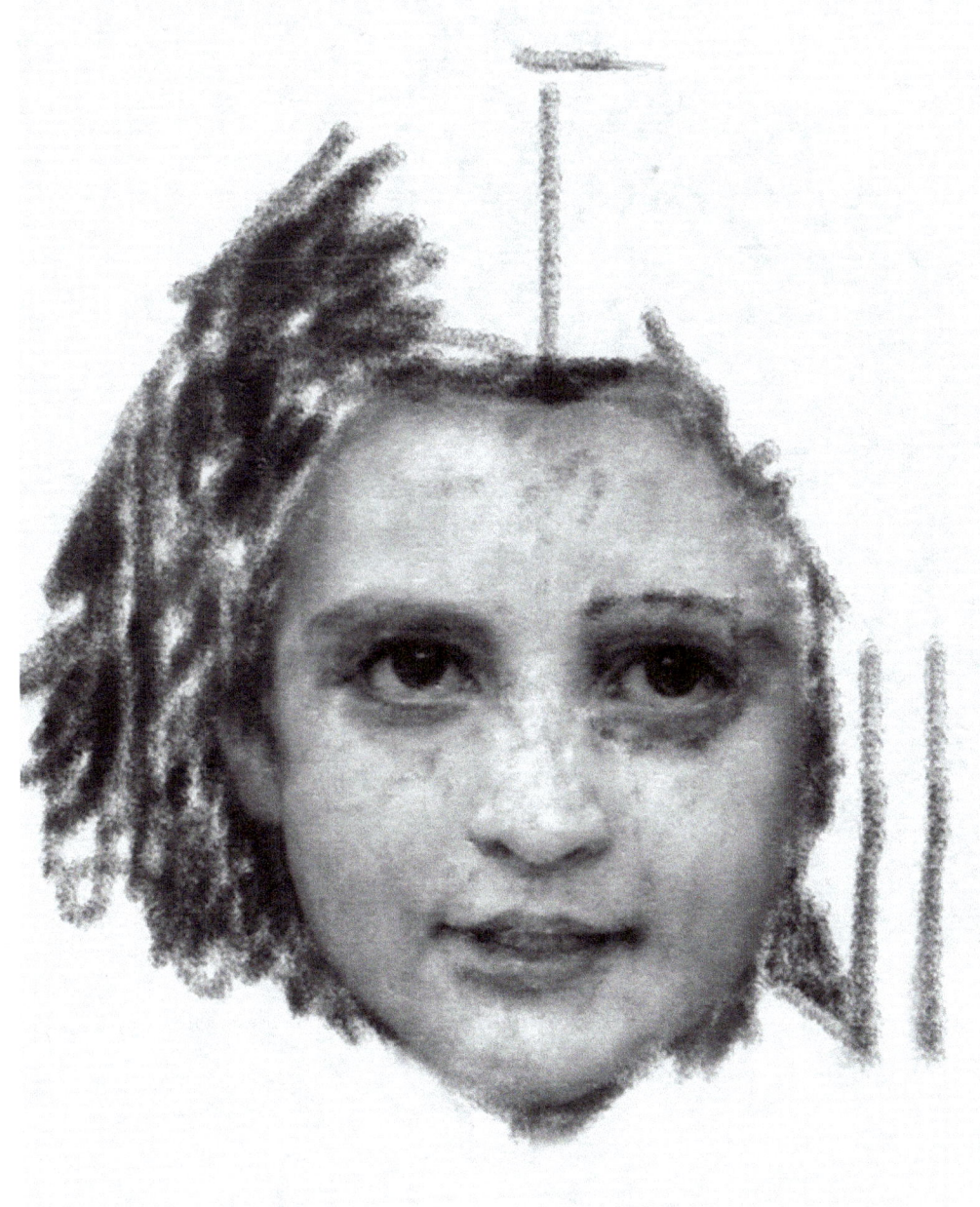

**You Can Draw Portraits:
Technical Drawing-Mastering an Exact Likeness** *(Drawing V)*

**STAGES FOR DRAWING THE PORTRAIT:
FINISHING THE HAIR AND NECK**

Continued

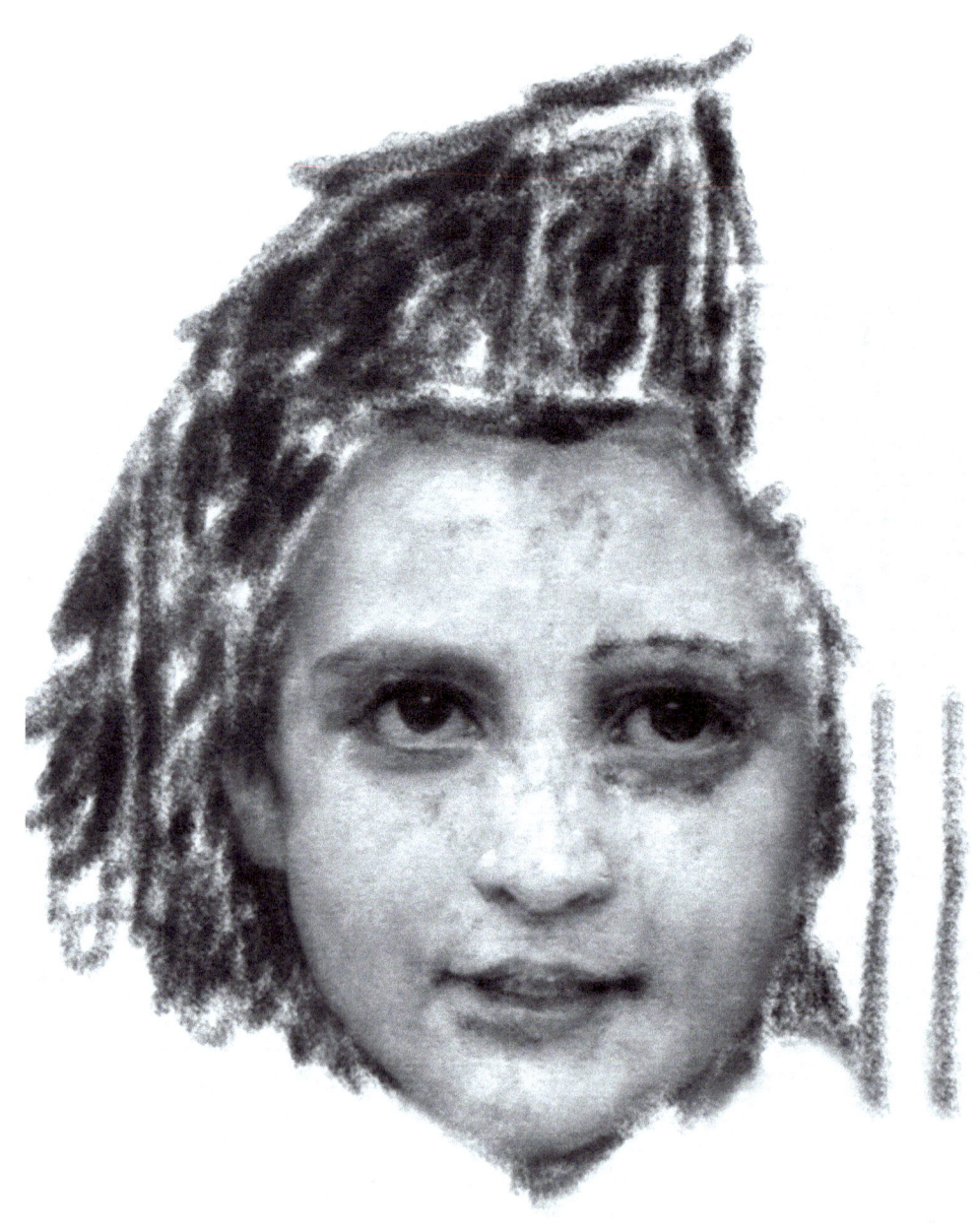

**You Can Draw Portraits:
Technical Drawing-Mastering an Exact Likeness** *(Drawing V)*

STAGES FOR DRAWING THE PORTRAIT: FINISHING THE HAIR AND NECK

Continued

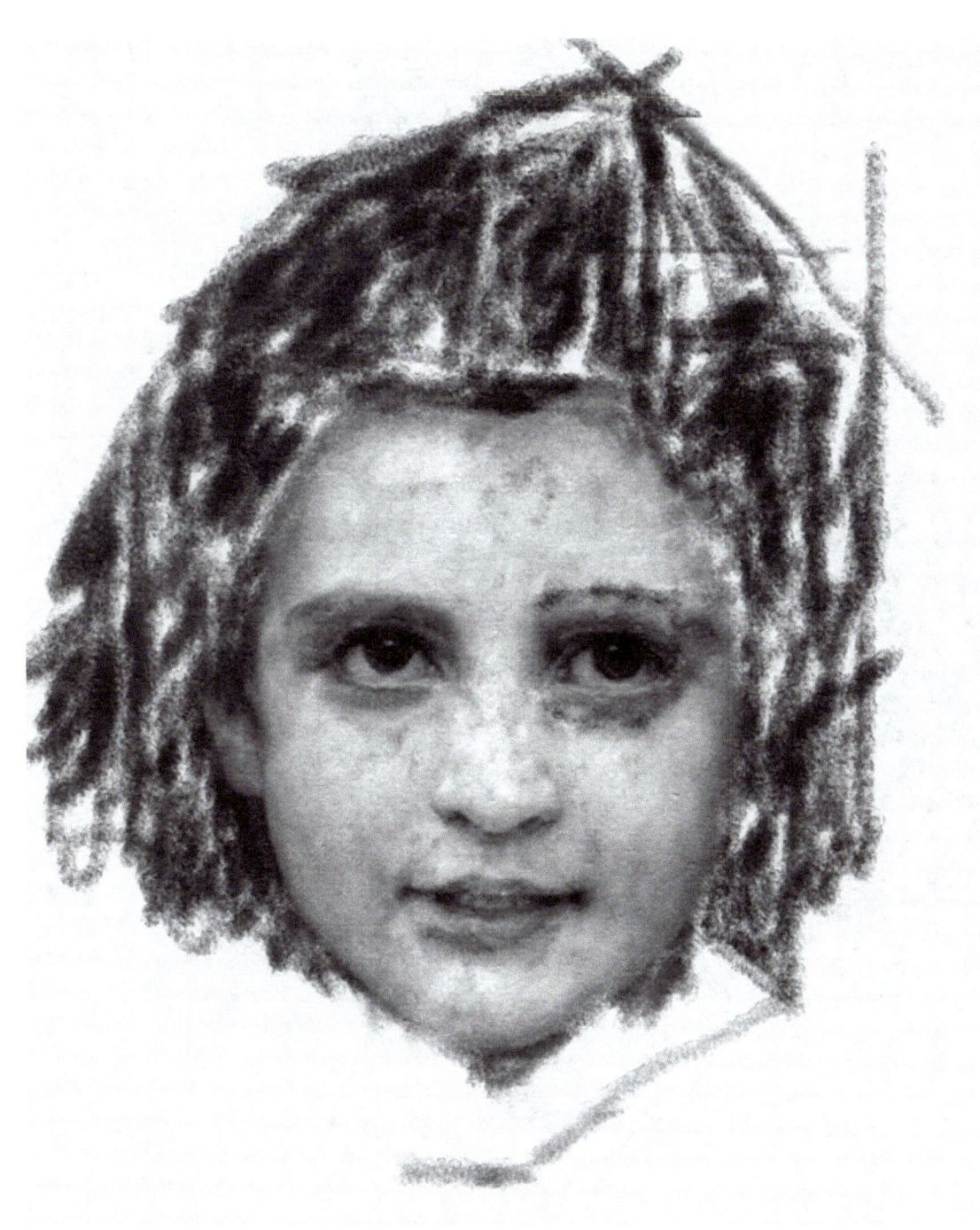

**You Can Draw Portraits:
Technical Drawing-Mastering an Exact Likeness**   *(Drawing V)*

**STAGES FOR DRAWING THE PORTRAIT:
FINISHING THE HAIR AND NECK**

Continued

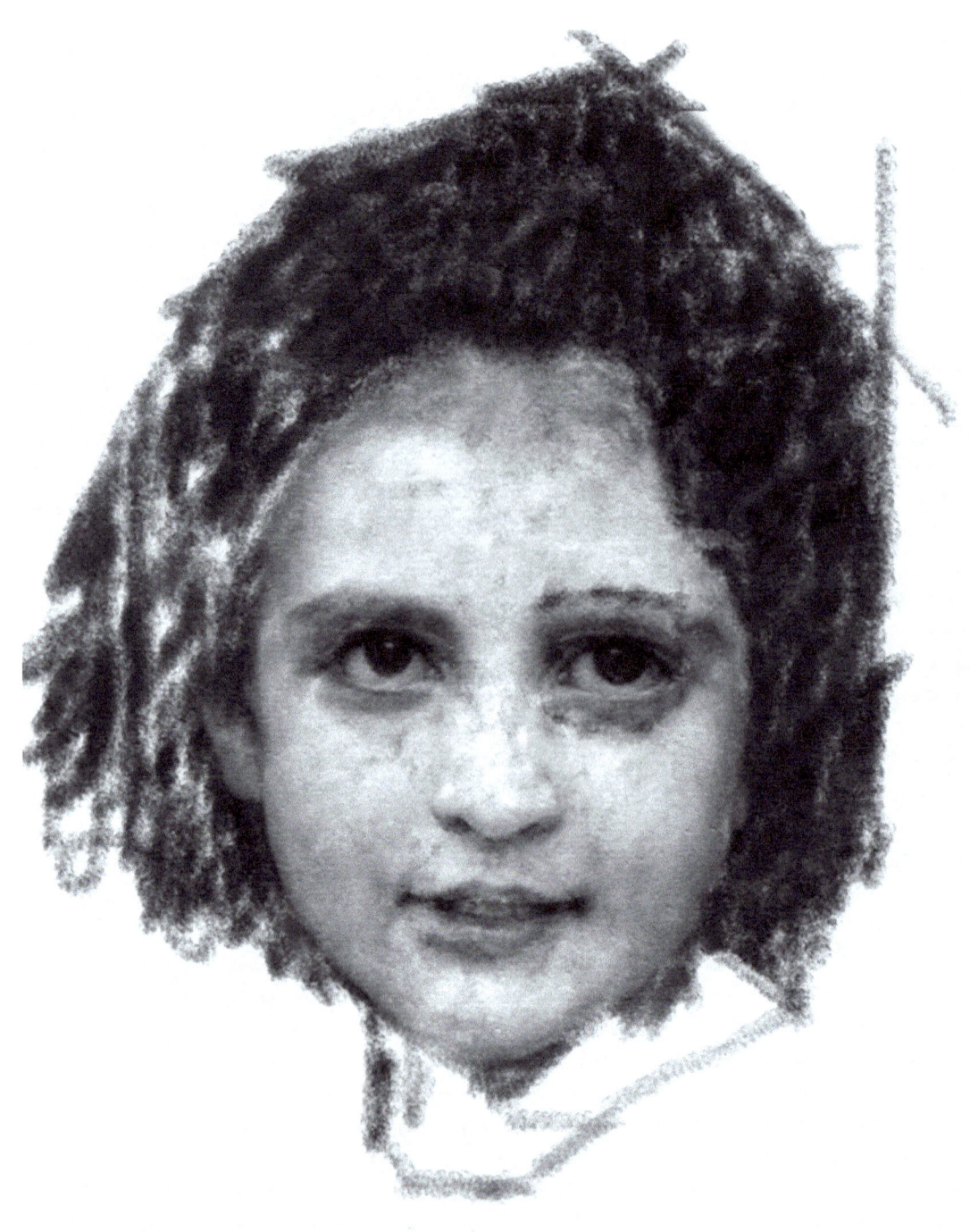

You Can Draw Portraits:
Technical Drawing-Mastering an Exact Likeness *(Drawing V)*

STAGES FOR DRAWING THE PORTRAIT:
FINISHING THE HAIR AND NECK

Continued

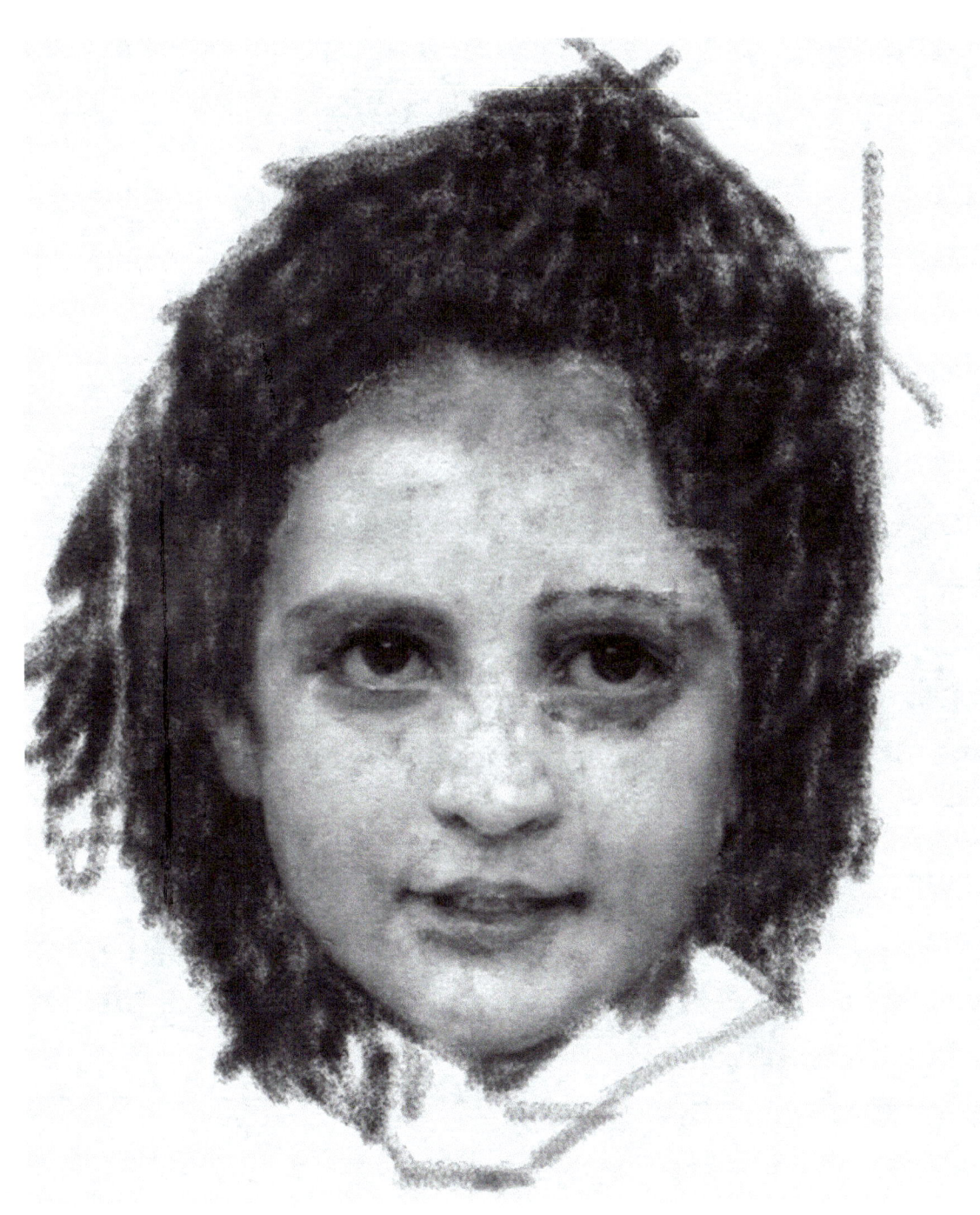

**You Can Draw Portraits:
Technical Drawing-Mastering an Exact Likeness** *(Drawing V)*

STAGES FOR DRAWING THE PORTRAIT: FINISHING THE HAIR AND NECK

Continued

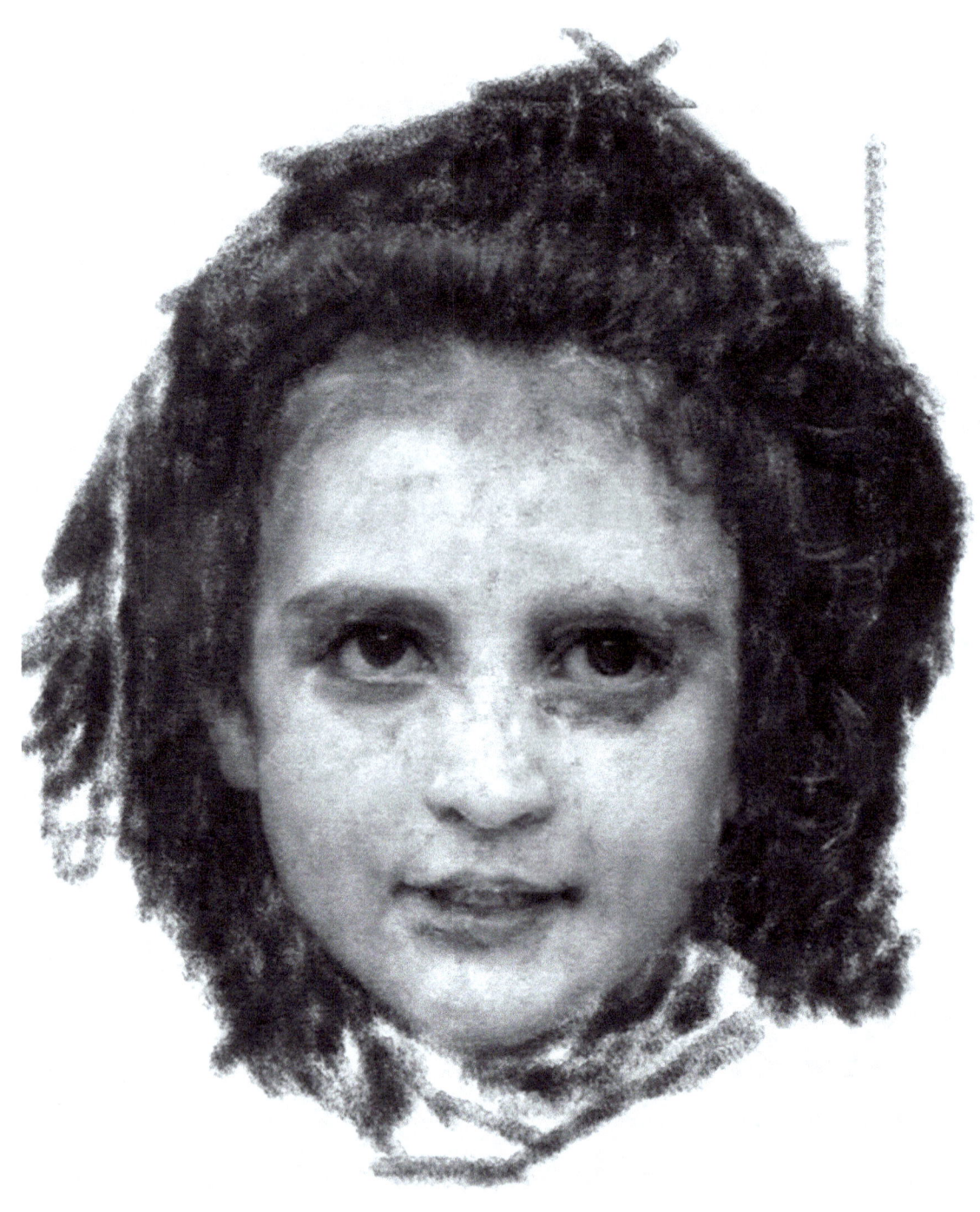

**You Can Draw Portraits:
Technical Drawing-Mastering an Exact Likeness** *(Drawing V)*

STAGES FOR DRAWING THE PORTRAIT: FINISHING THE HAIR AND NECK

Continued

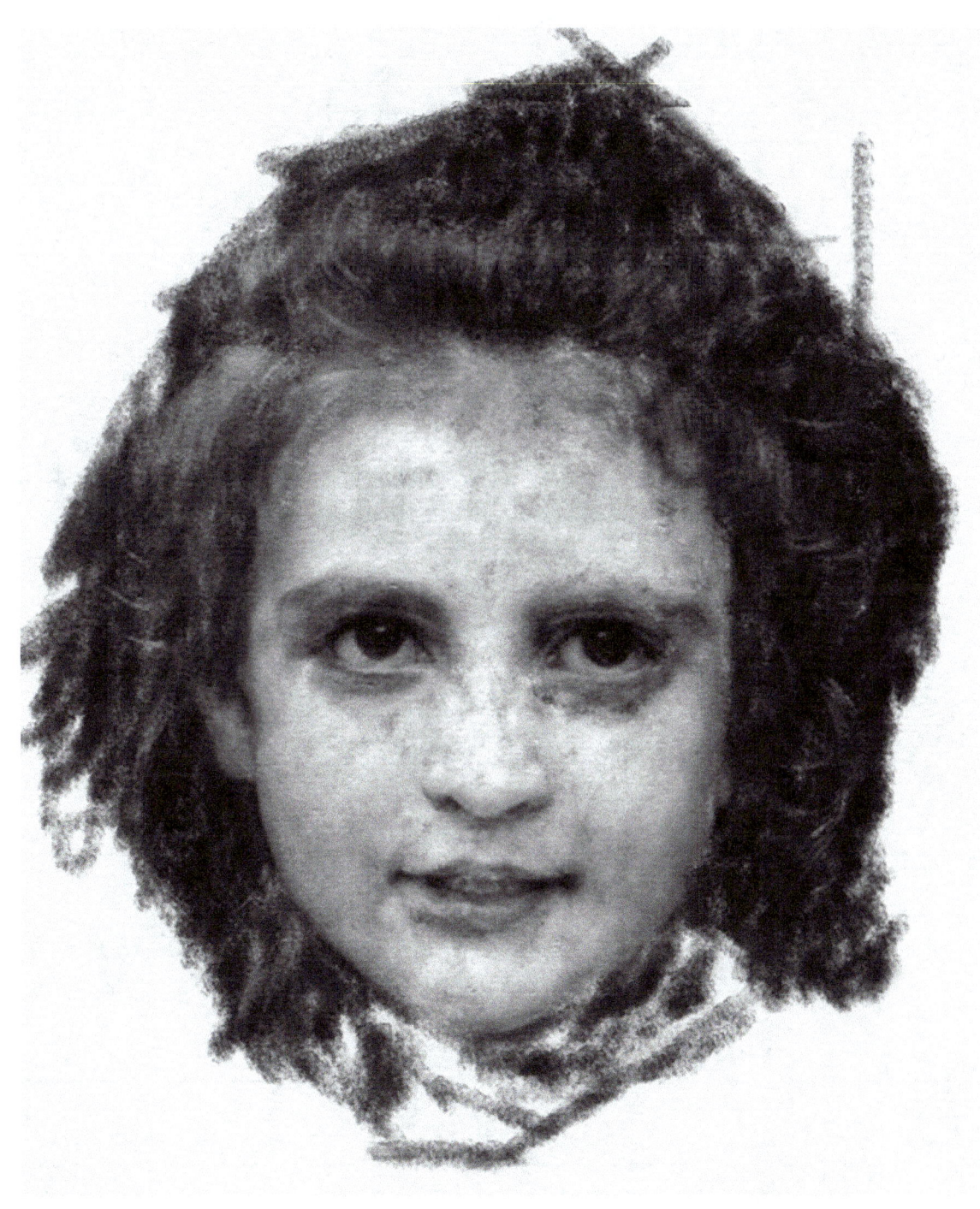

You Can Draw Portraits:
Technical Drawing-Mastering an Exact Likeness *(Drawing V)*

STAGES FOR DRAWING THE PORTRAIT: FINISHING THE HAIR AND NECK

Continued

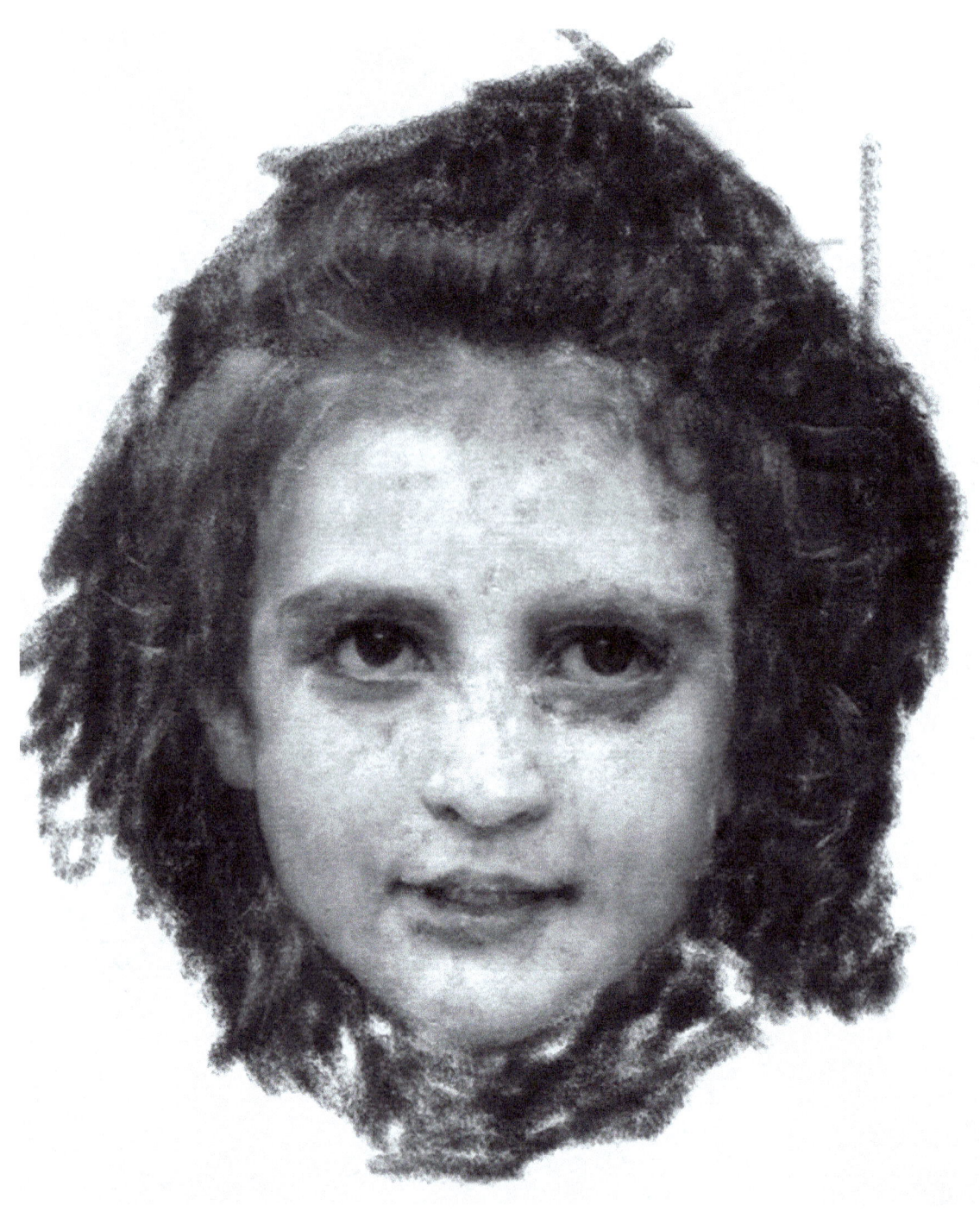

**You Can Draw Portraits:
Technical Drawing–Mastering an Exact Likeness** *(Drawing V)*

STAGES FOR DRAWING THE PORTRAIT: FINISHING THE HAIR AND NECK

Continued

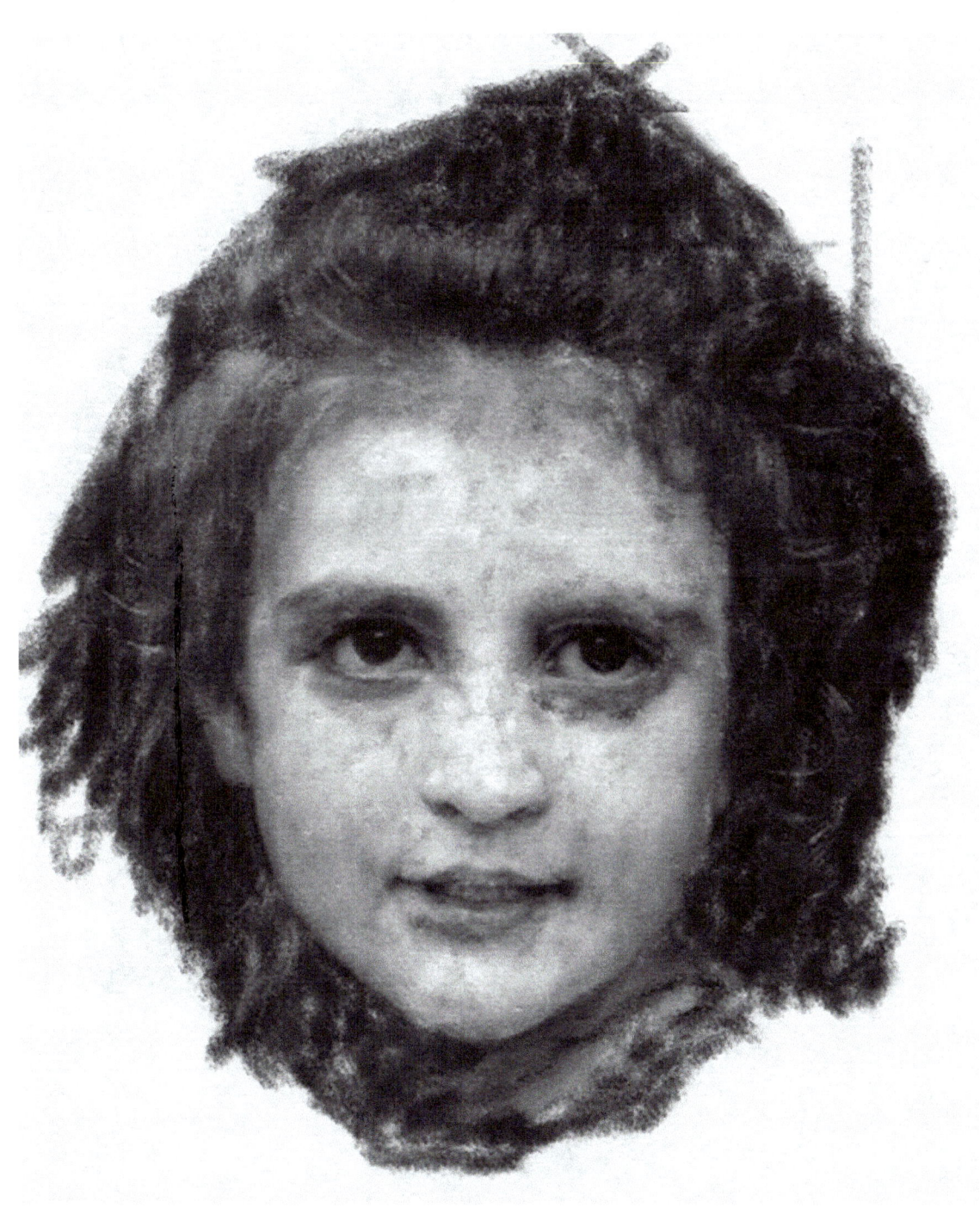

You Can Draw Portraits:
Technical Drawing-Mastering an Exact Likeness *(Drawing V)*

STAGES FOR DRAWING THE PORTRAIT: FINISHING THE HAIR AND NECK

Continued

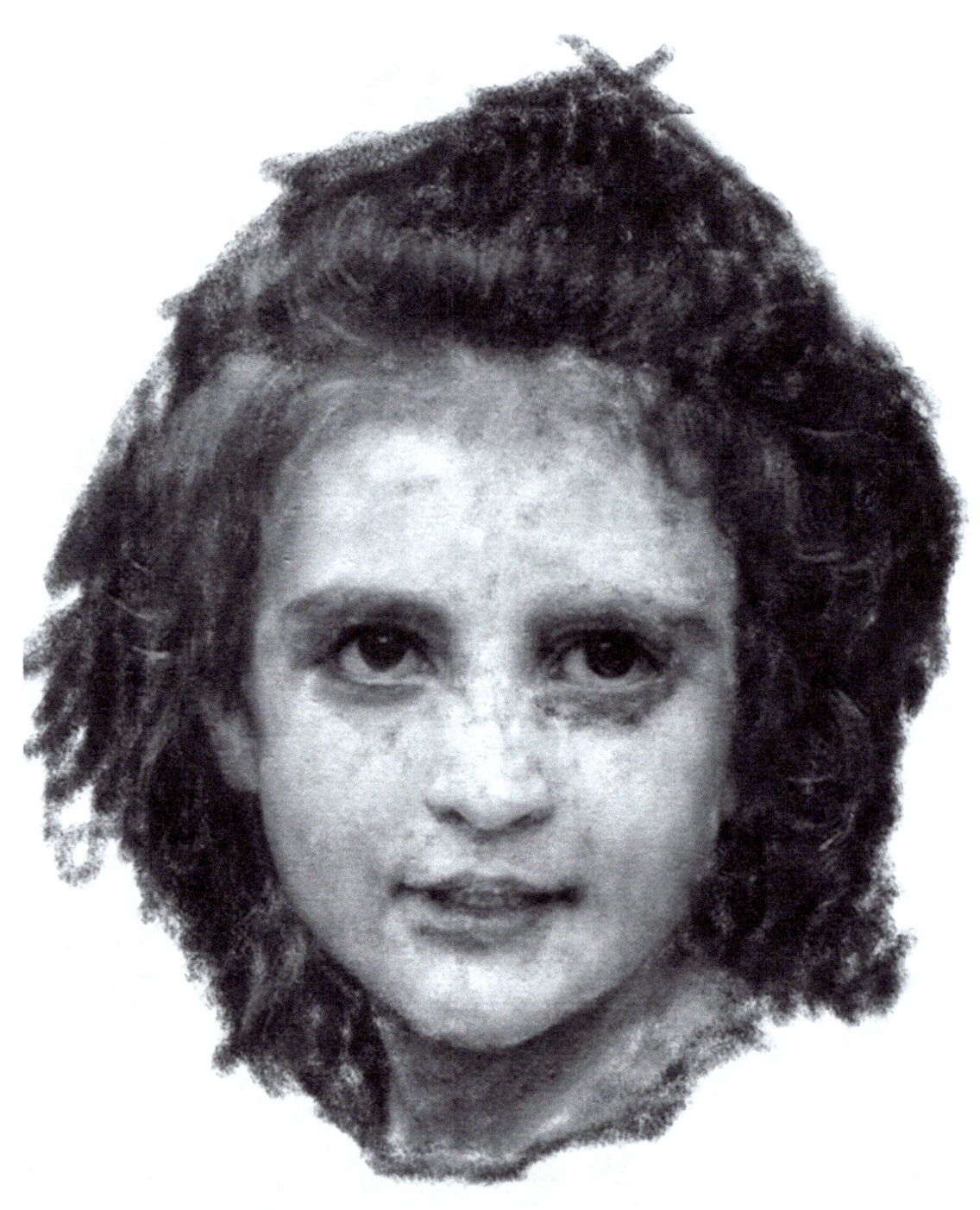

**You Can Draw Portraits:
Technical Drawing-Mastering an Exact Likeness**   *(Drawing V)*

STAGES FOR DRAWING THE PORTRAIT: FINISHING THE HAIR AND NECK

Continued

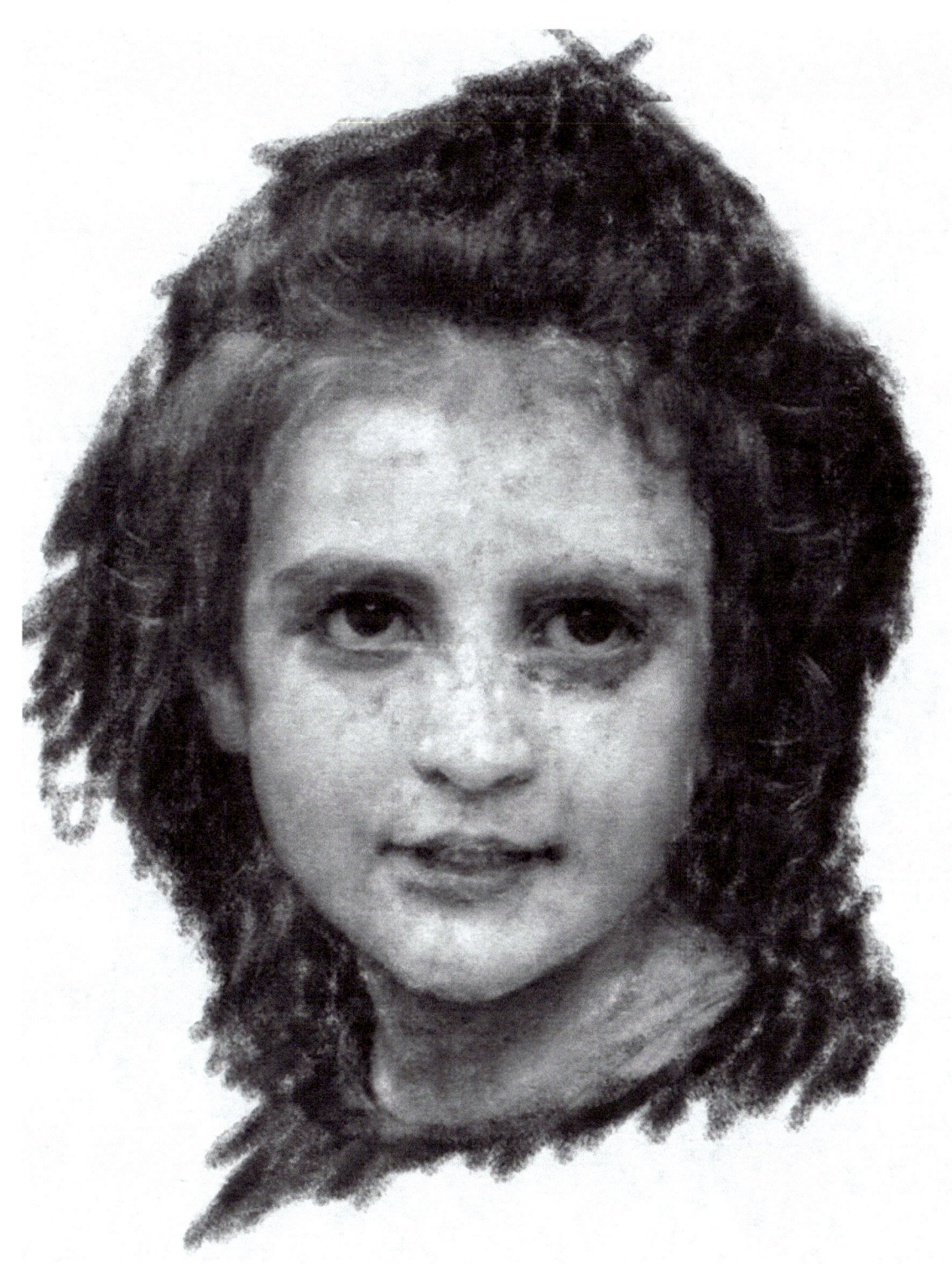

You Can Draw Portraits:
Technical Drawing-Mastering an Exact Likeness *(Drawing V)*

STAGES FOR DRAWING THE PORTRAIT: FINISHING THE HAIR AND NECK

Continued

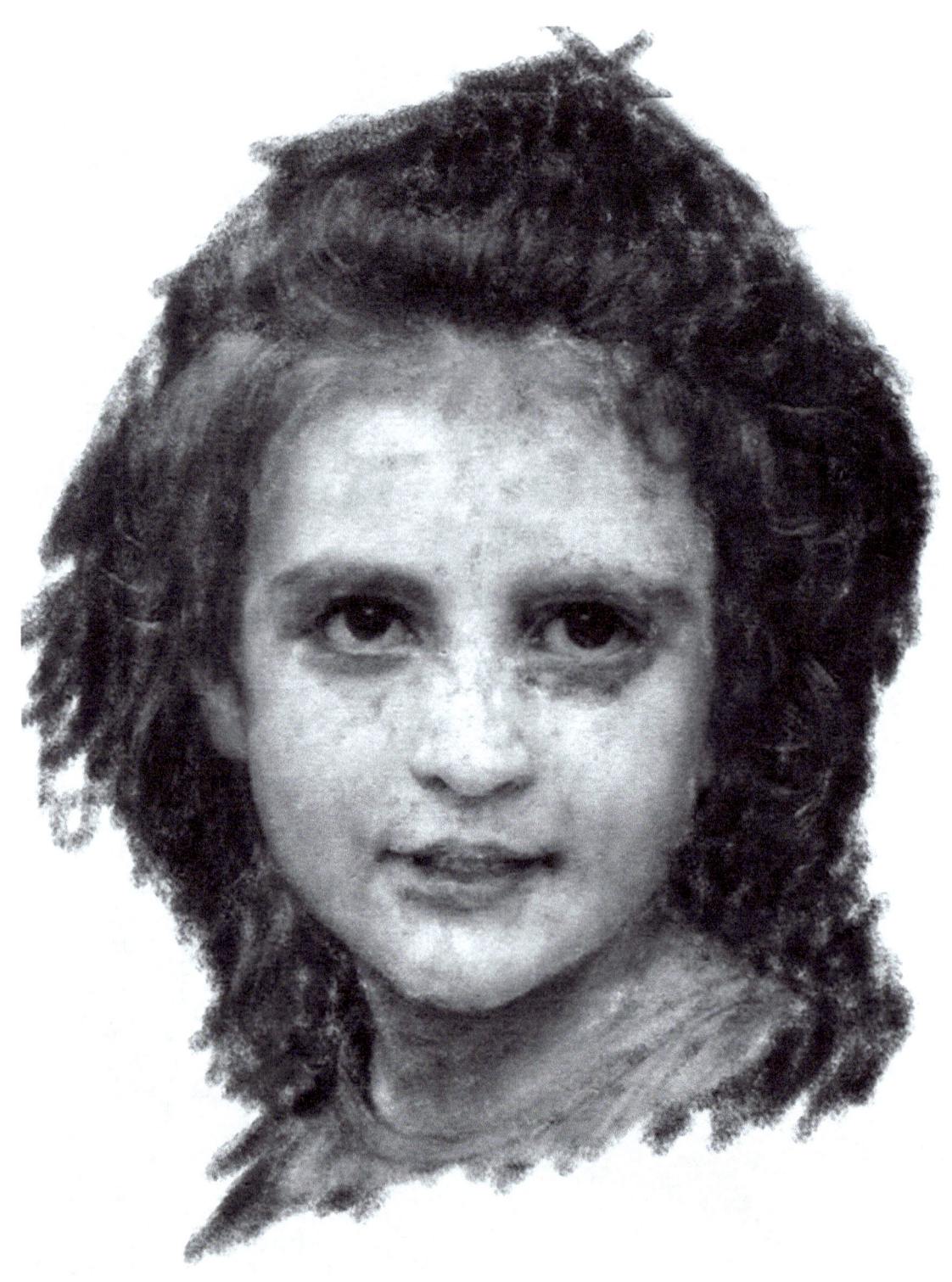

You Can Draw Portraits: Technical Drawing-Mastering an Exact Likeness *(Drawing V)*

STAGES FOR DRAWING THE PORTRAIT: FINISHING THE HAIR AND NECK

Continued

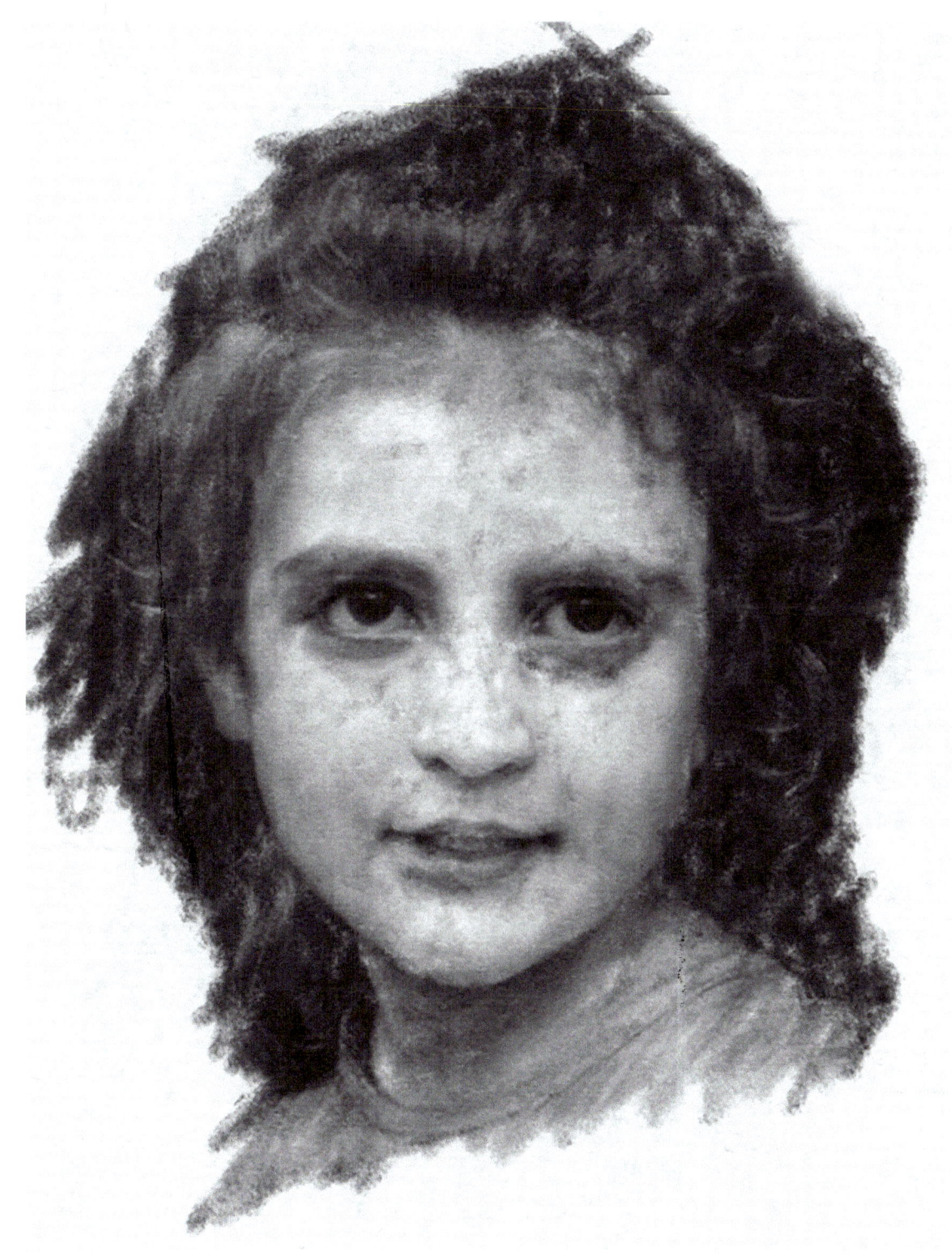

You Can Draw Portraits:
Technical Drawing-Mastering an Exact Likeness *(Drawing V)*

STAGES FOR DRAWING THE PORTRAIT:
FINISHING THE HAIR AND NECK

Continued

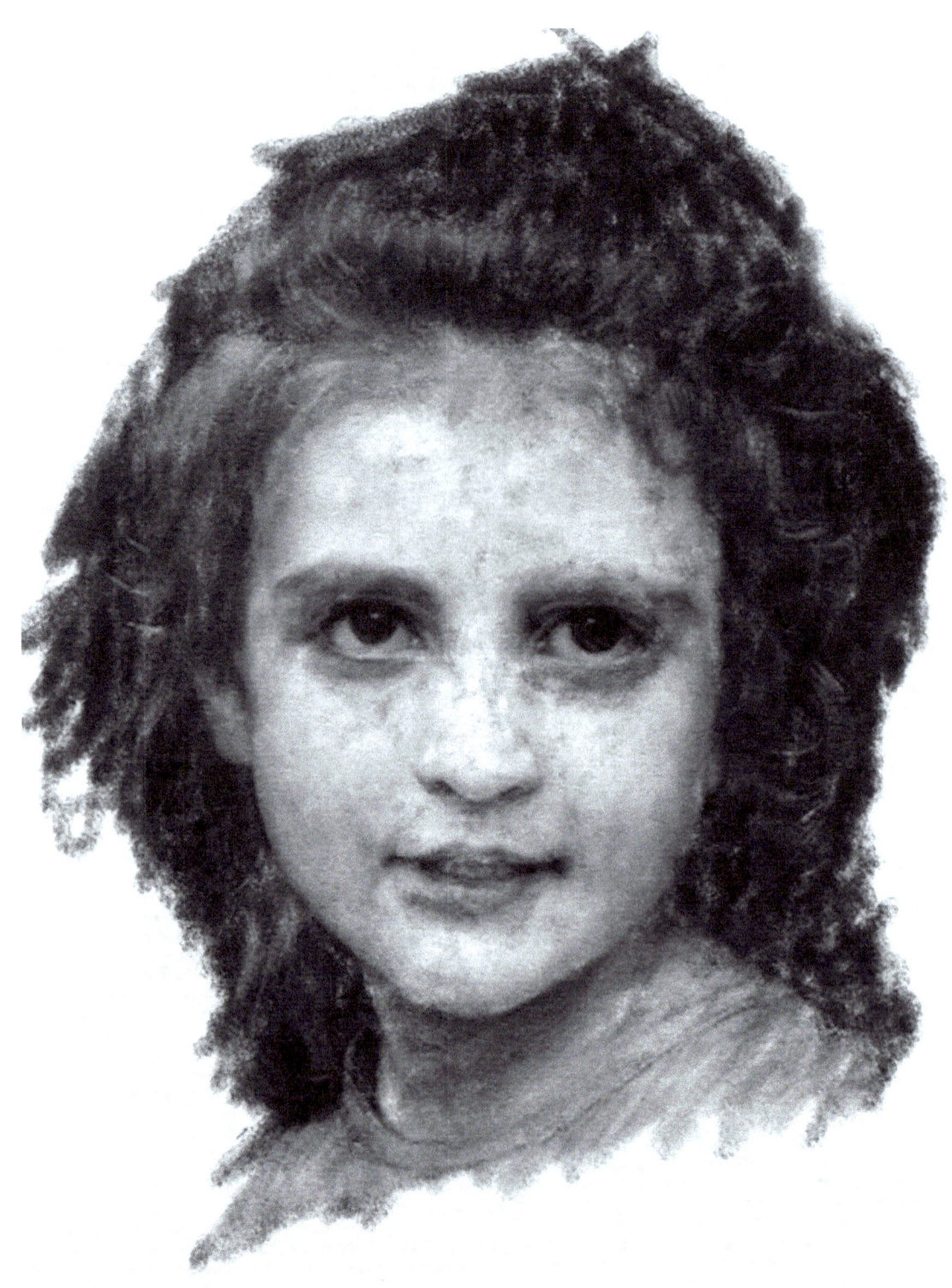

**You Can Draw Portraits:
Technical Drawing-Mastering an Exact Likeness** *(Drawing V)*

STAGES FOR DRAWING THE PORTRAIT: FINISHING THE HAIR AND NECK

Continued

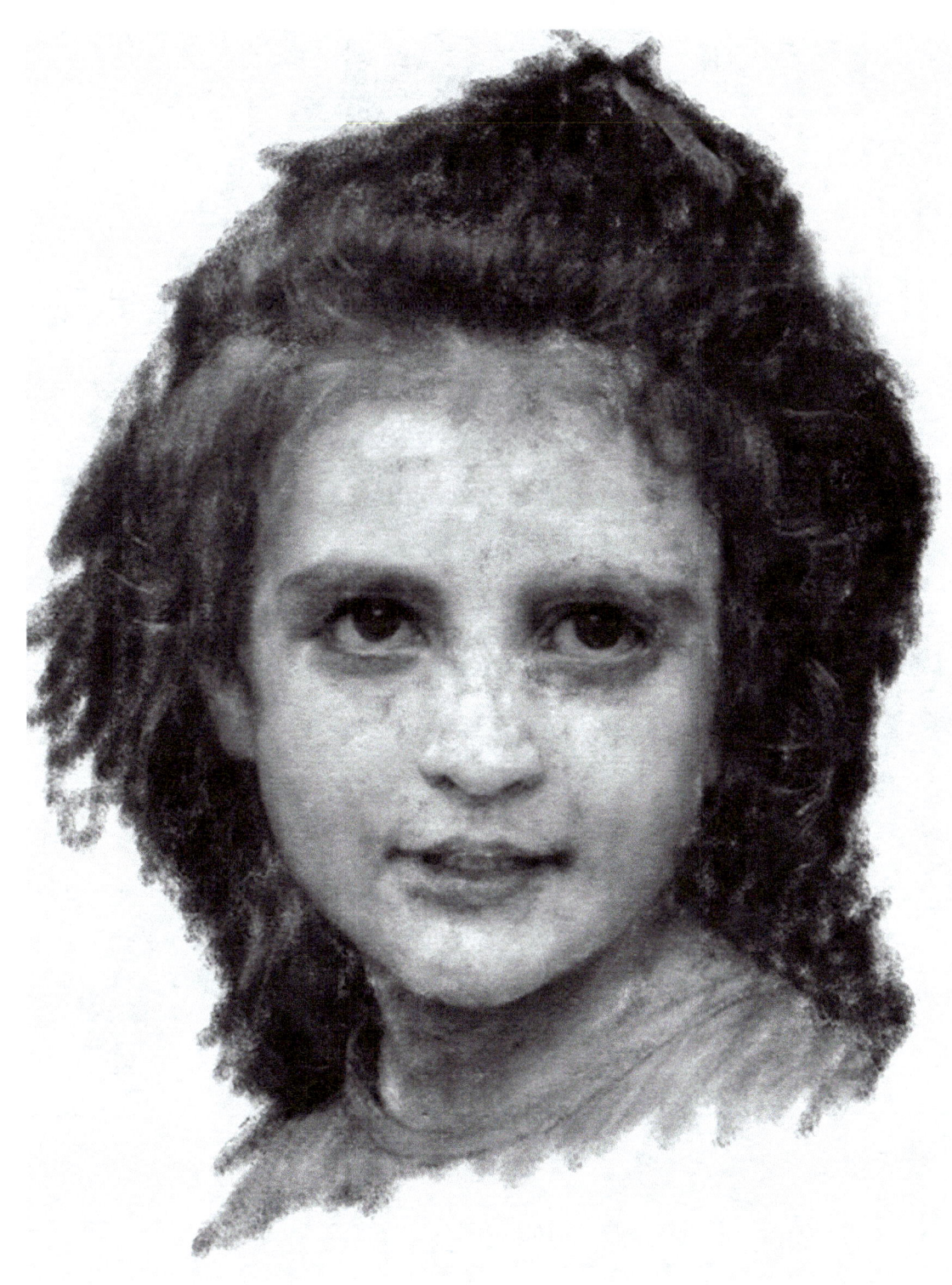

You Can Draw Portraits:
Technical Drawing-Mastering an Exact Likeness *(Drawing V)*

STAGES FOR DRAWING THE PORTRAIT: FINISHING THE HAIR AND NECK

Continued

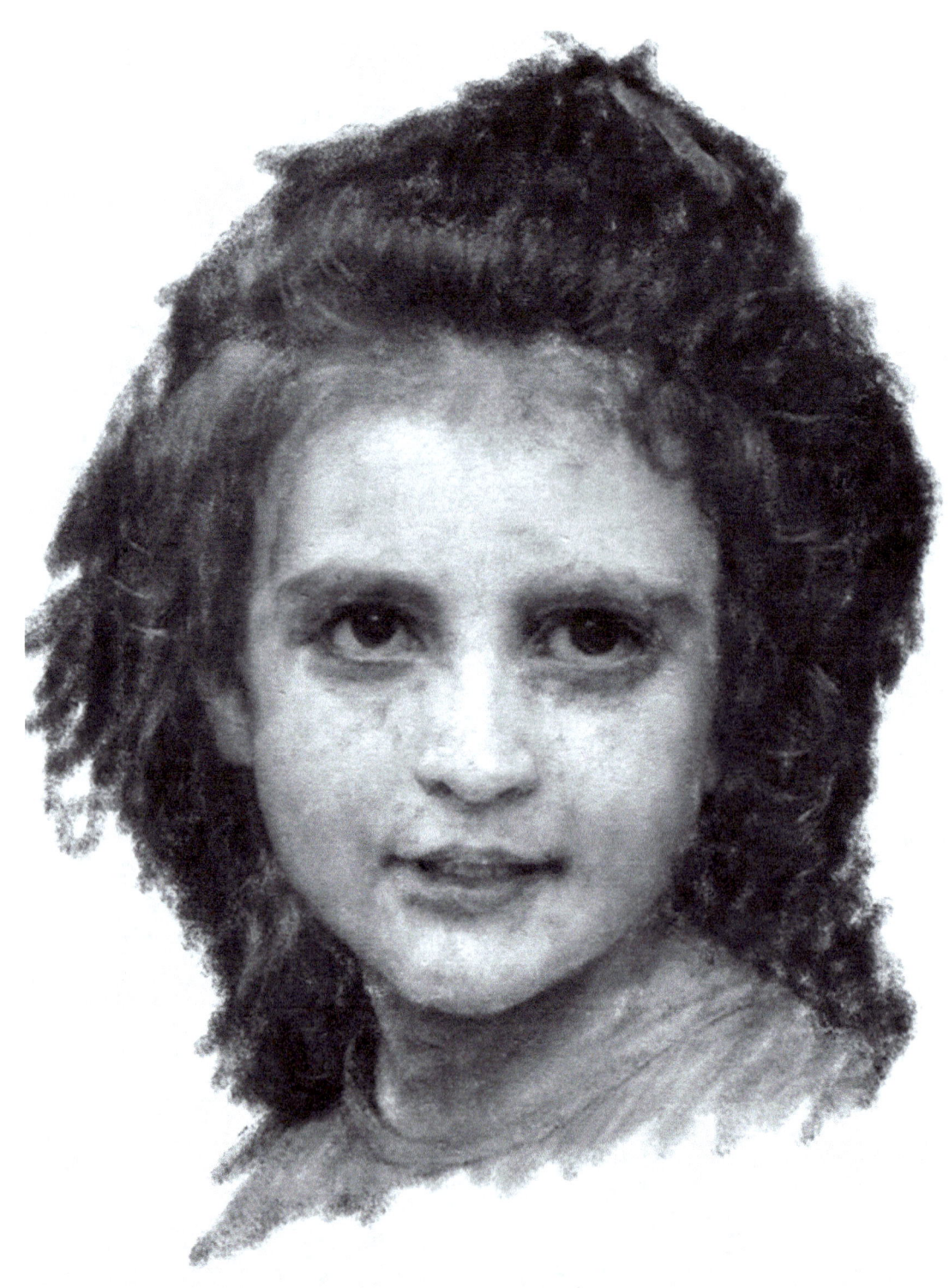

**You Can Draw Portraits:
Technical Drawing-Mastering an Exact Likeness** *(Drawing V)*

STAGES FOR DRAWING THE PORTRAIT: FINISHING THE HAIR AND NECK

Continued

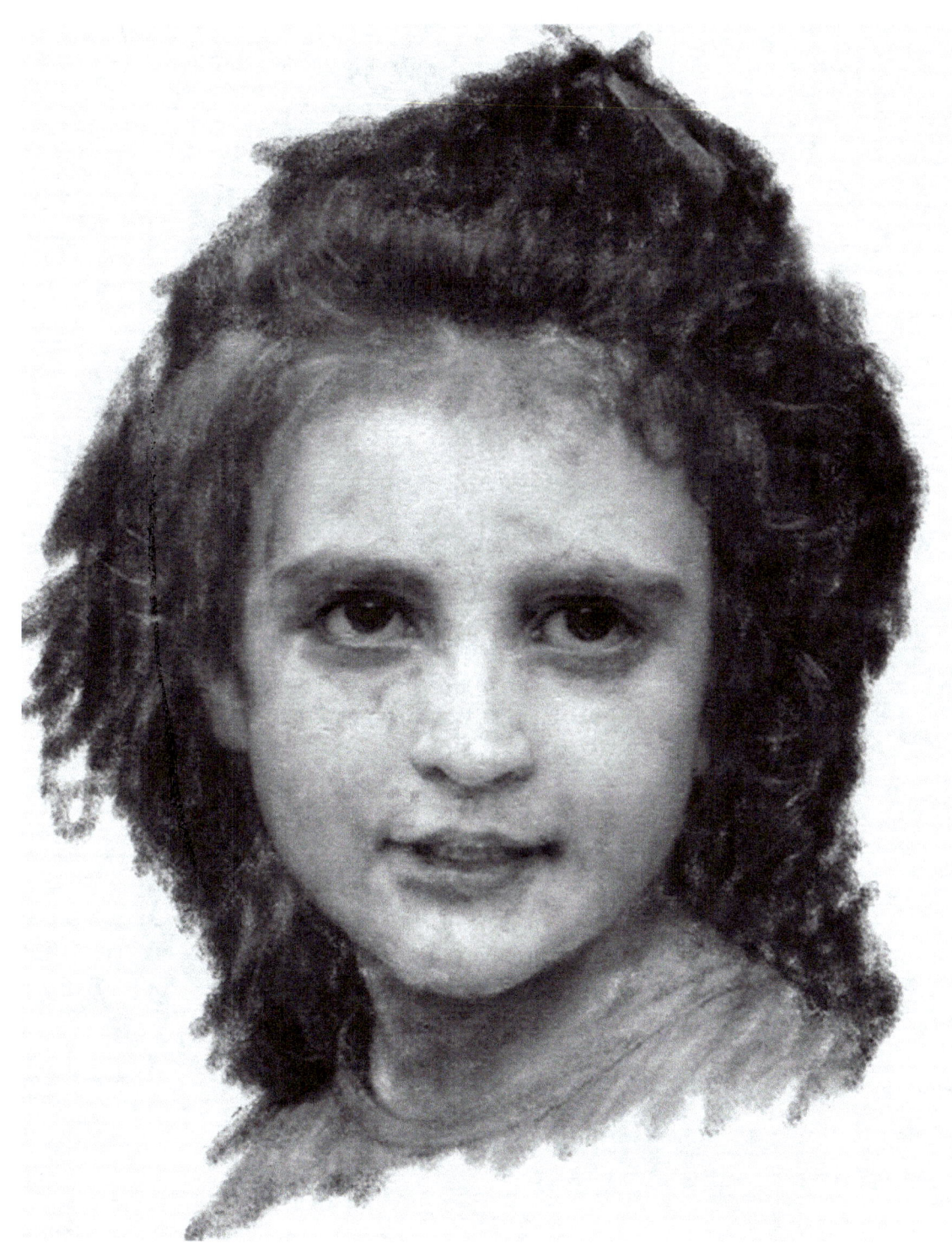

**You Can Draw Portraits:
Technical Drawing-Mastering an Exact Likeness** *(Drawing V)*

**STAGES FOR DRAWING THE PORTRAIT:
FINISHING THE HAIR AND NECK**

Continued

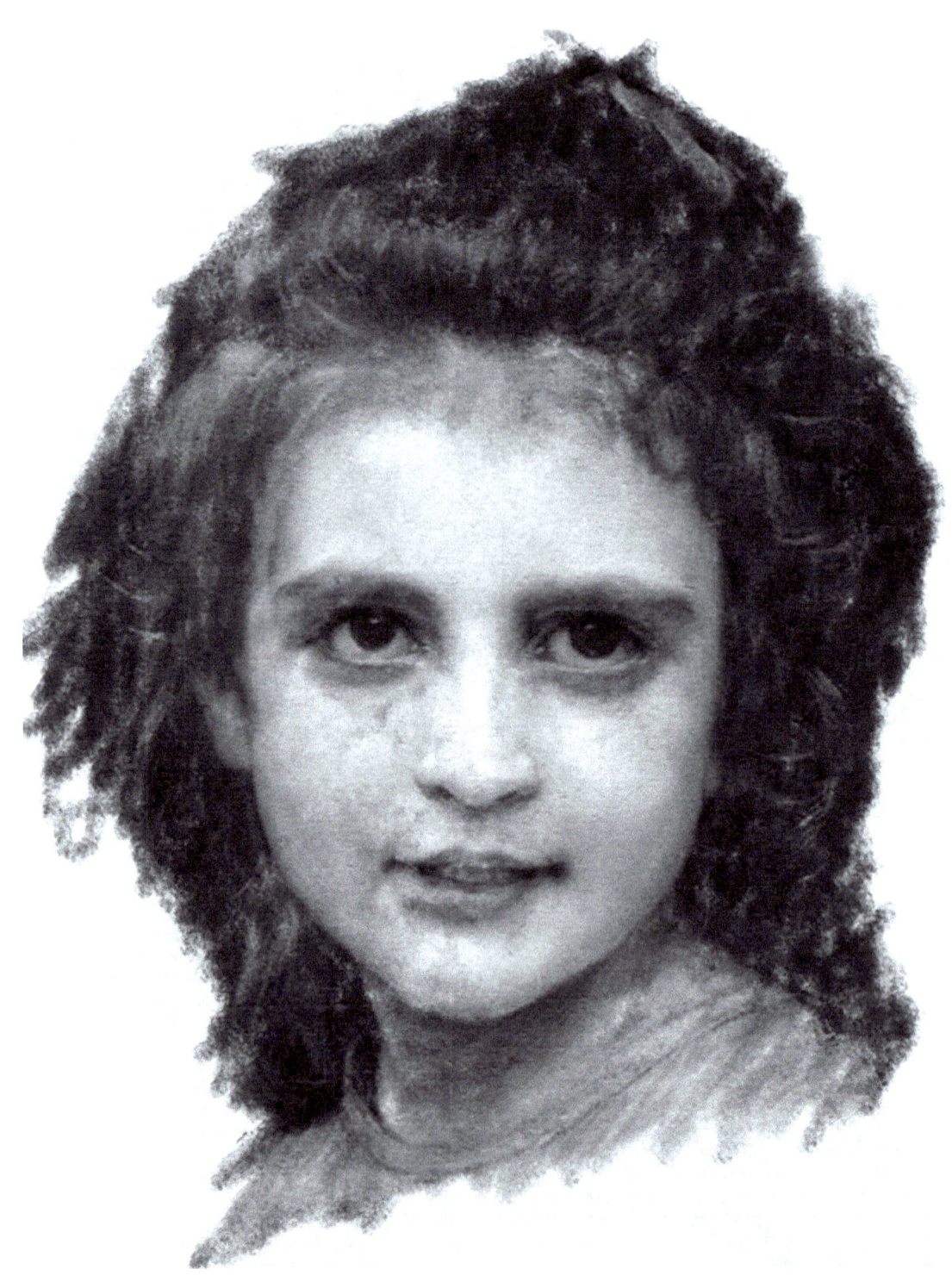

**You Can Draw Portraits:
Technical Drawing-Mastering an Exact Likeness** *(Drawing V)*

STAGES FOR DRAWING THE PORTRAIT: FINISHING THE HAIR AND NECK

Continued

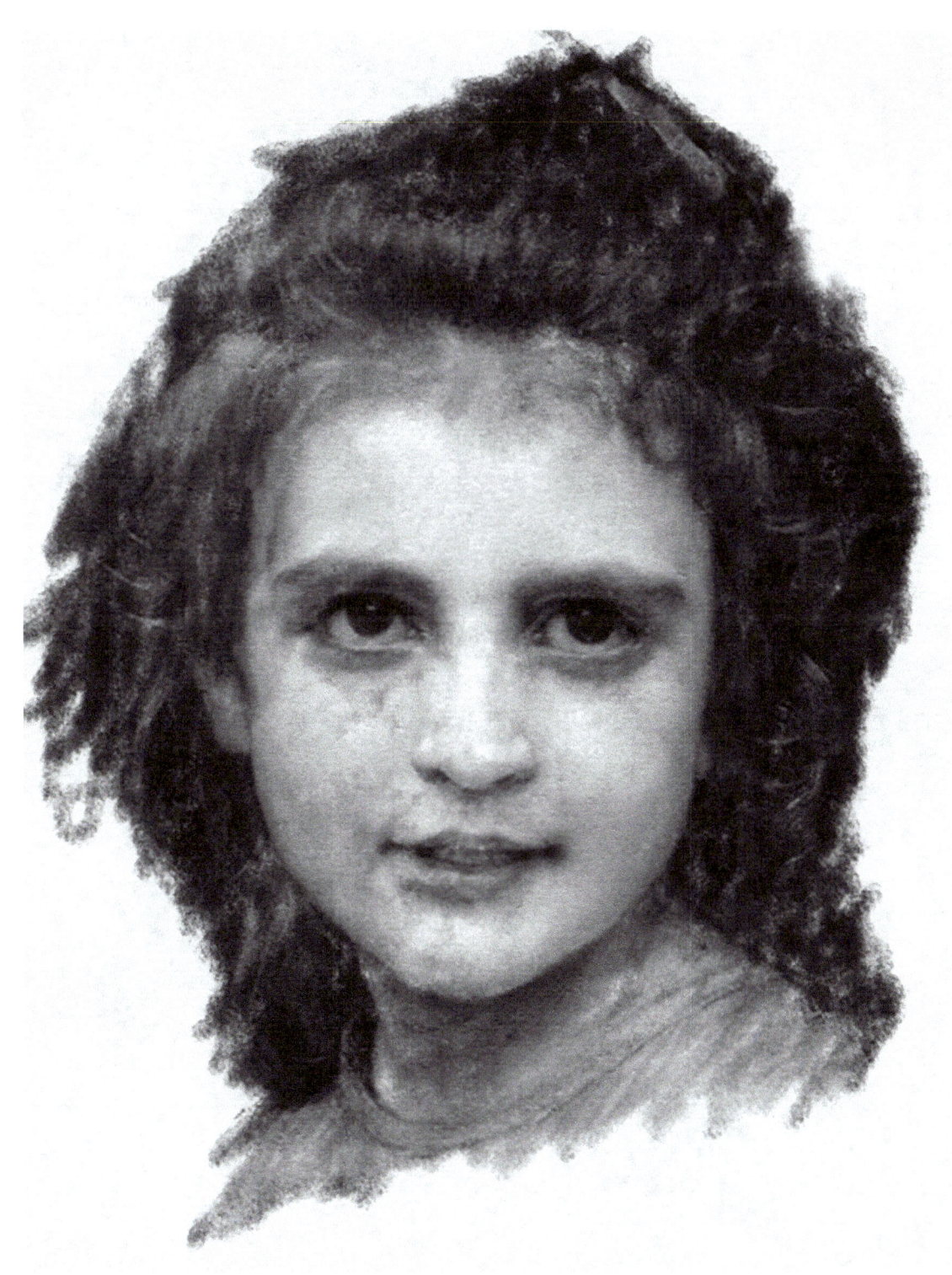

You Can Draw Portraits:
Technical Drawing-Mastering an Exact Likeness *(Drawing V)*

STAGES FOR DRAWING THE PORTRAIT: FINISHING THE HAIR AND NECK

Continued

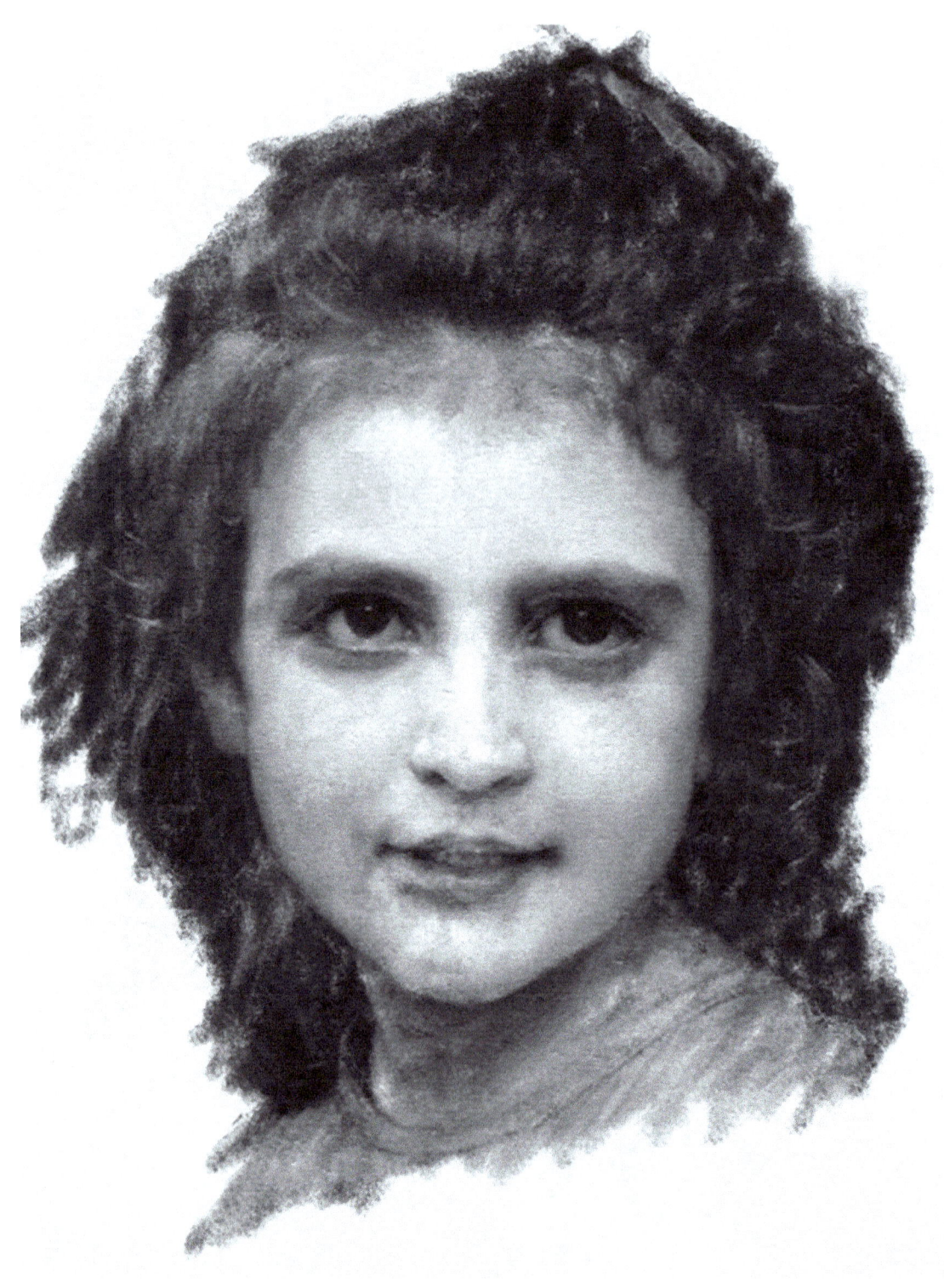

**You Can Draw Portraits:
Technical Drawing-Mastering an Exact Likeness** *(Drawing V)*

STAGES FOR DRAWING THE PORTRAIT: FINISHING THE HAIR AND NECK

Continued

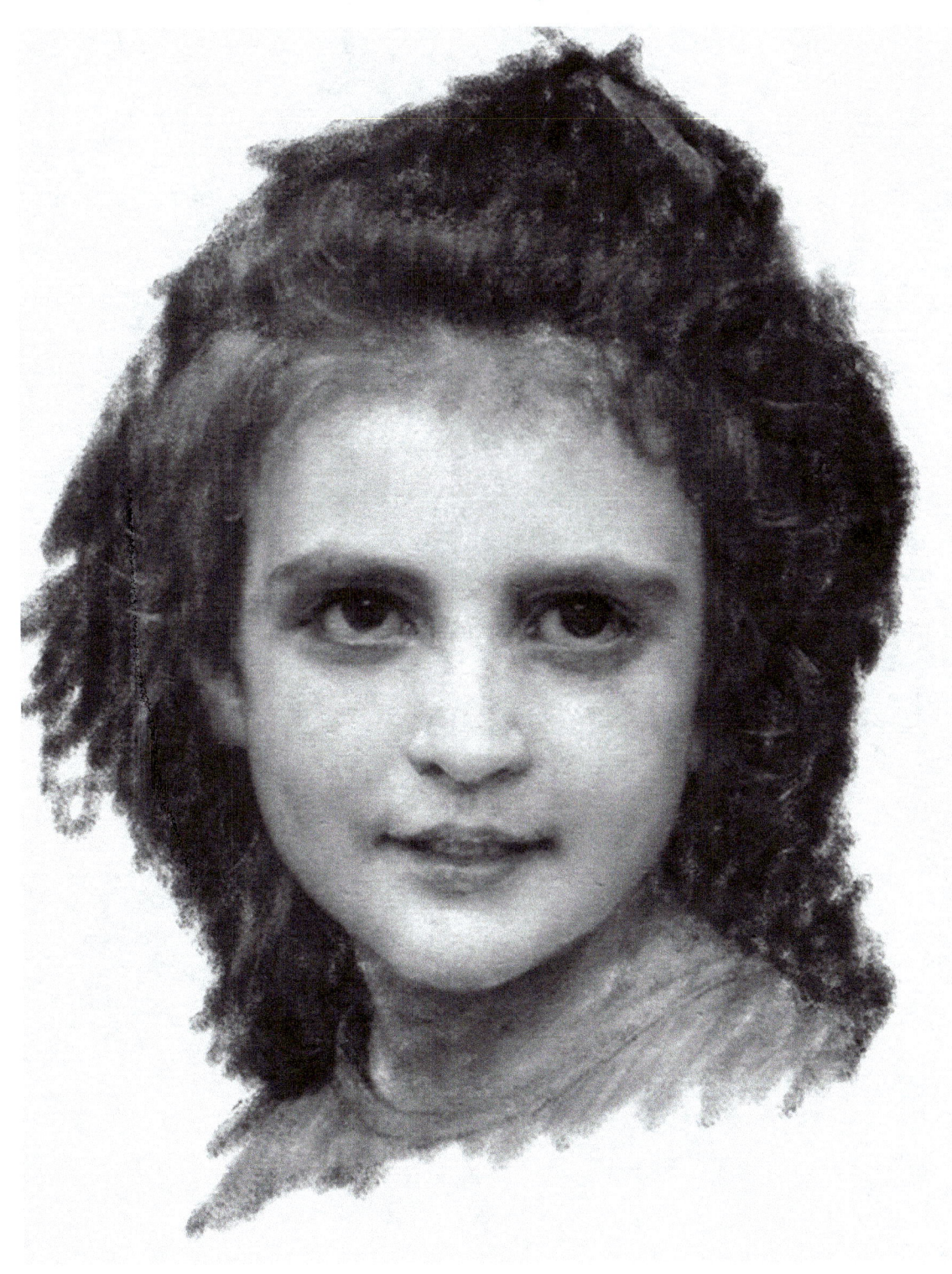

You Can Draw Portraits:
Technical Drawing-Mastering an Exact Likeness *(Drawing V)*

STAGES FOR DRAWING THE PORTRAIT: FINISHING THE HAIR AND NECK

Continued

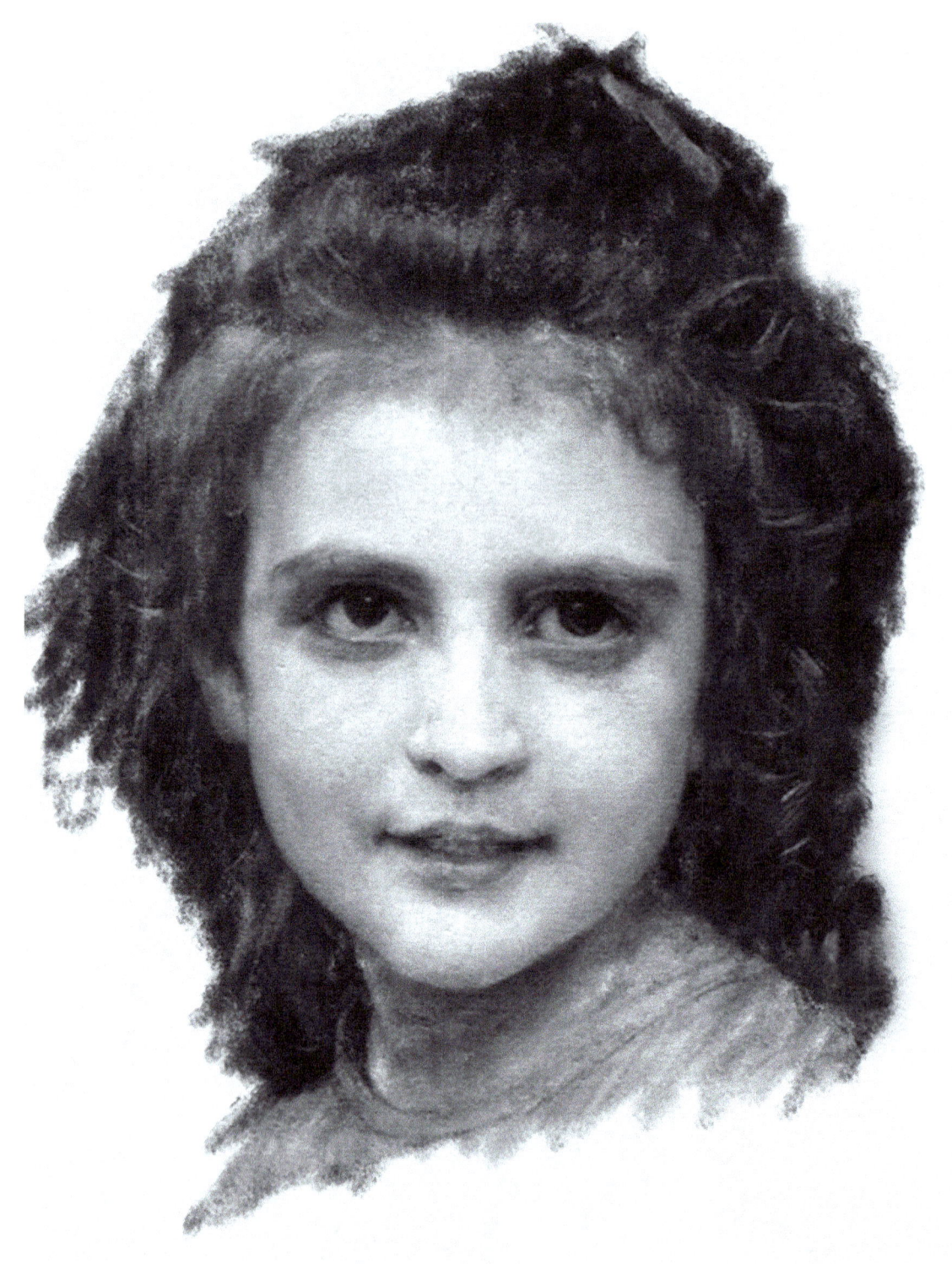

You Can Draw Portraits:
Technical Drawing-Mastering an Exact Likeness *(Drawing V)*

STAGES FOR DRAWING THE PORTRAIT: FINISHING THE HAIR AND NECK

Continued

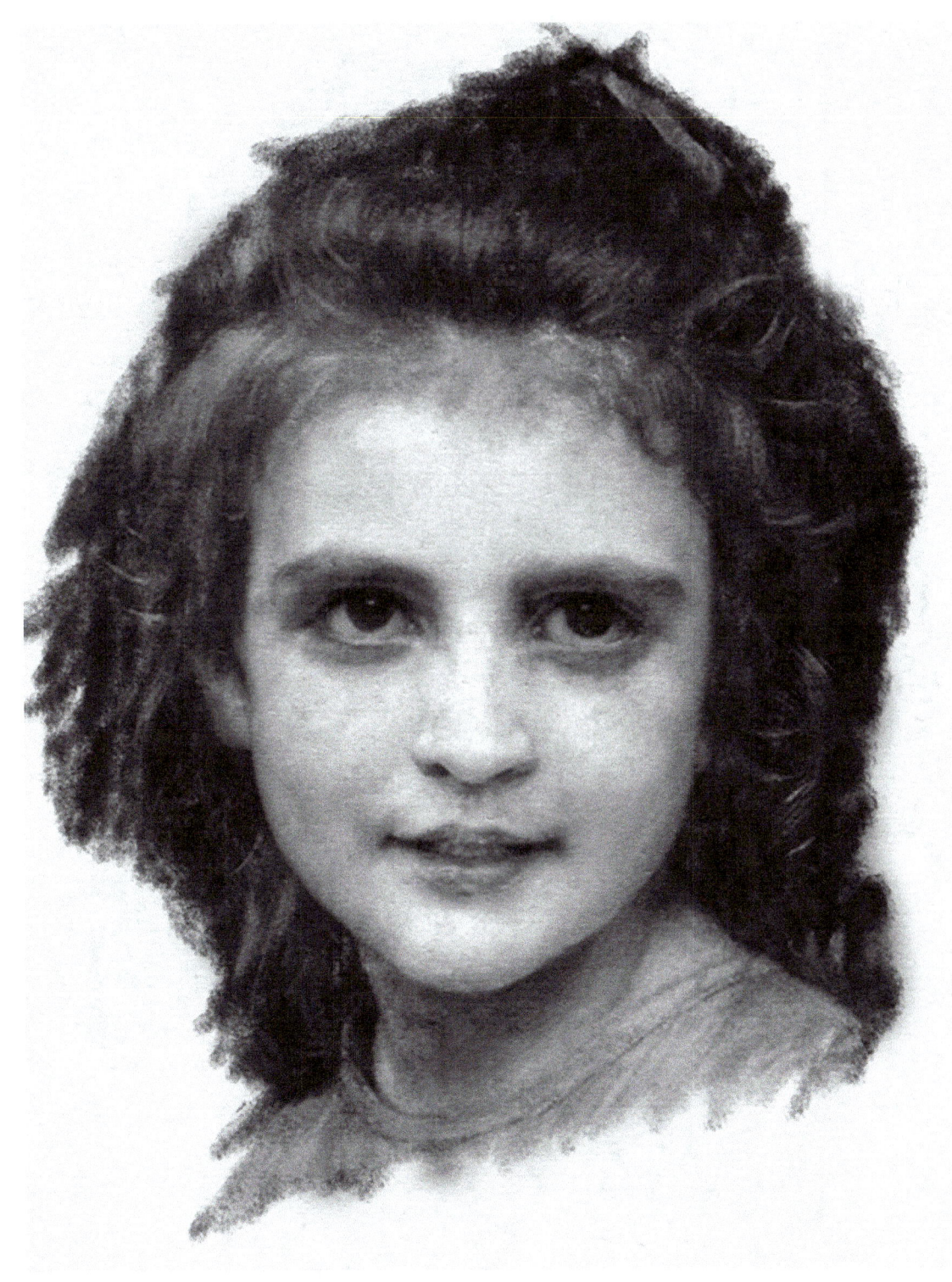

**You Can Draw Portraits:
Technical Drawing-Mastering an Exact Likeness** *(Drawing V)*

STAGES FOR DRAWING THE PORTRAIT: FINISHING THE HAIR AND NECK

Continued

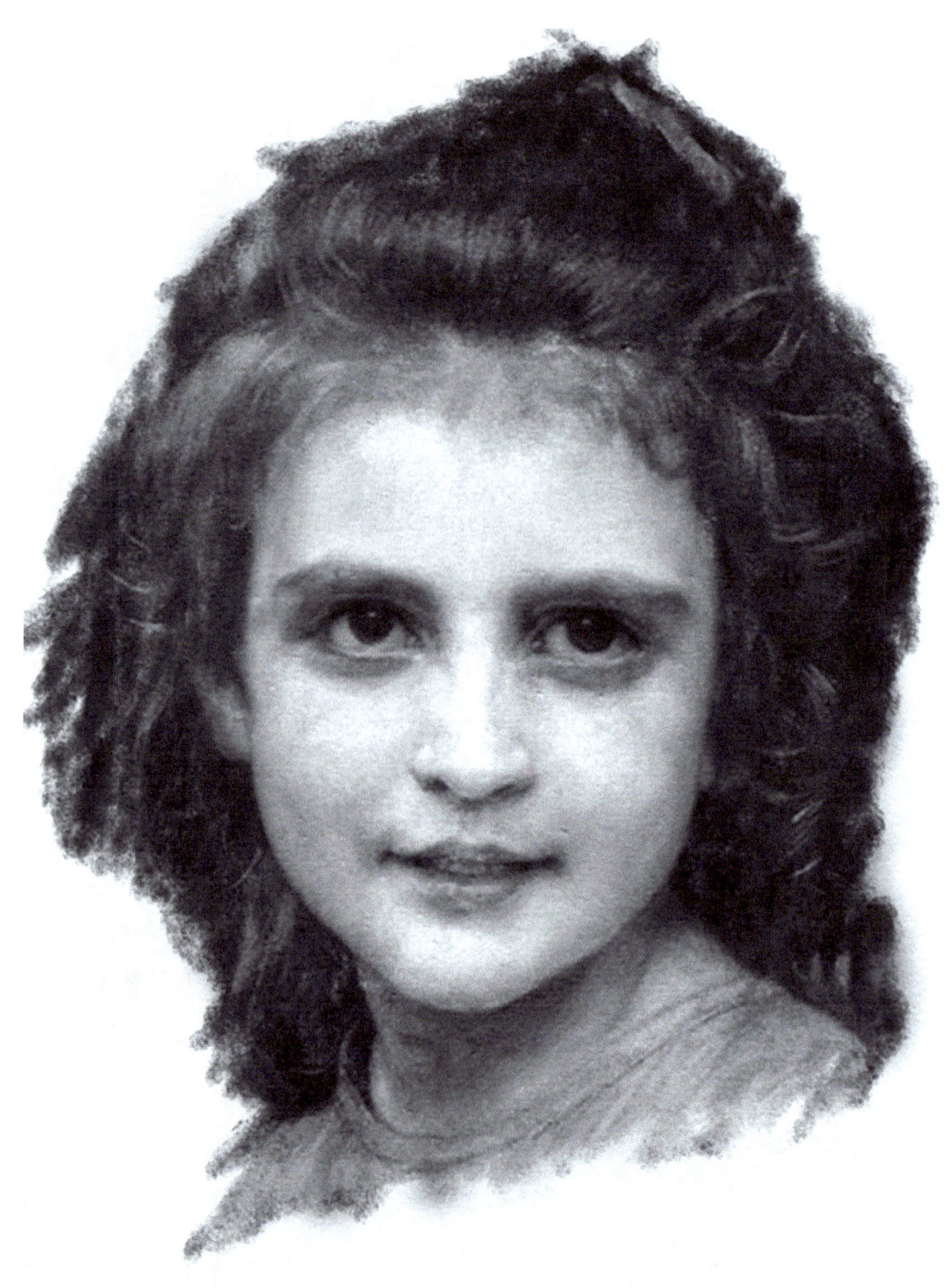

You Can Draw Portraits:
Technical Drawing-Mastering an Exact Likeness *(Drawing V)*

STAGES FOR DRAWING THE PORTRAIT: FINISHING THE HAIR AND NECK

Continued

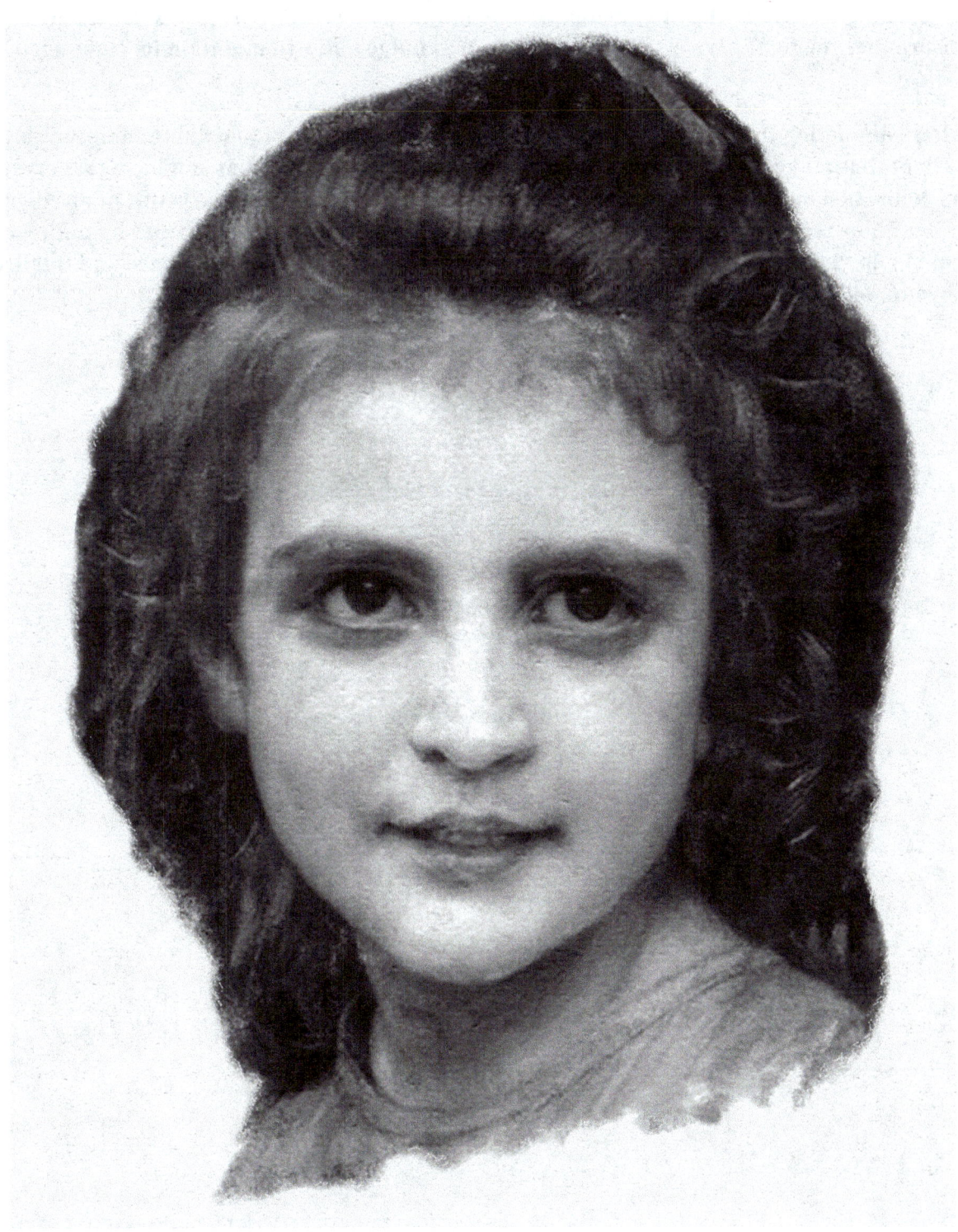

You Can Draw Portraits:
Technical Drawing-Mastering an Exact Likeness *(Drawing V)*

In this stage of the hair and neck, notice that we are also paying attention to the details that make up the textures and contours of the face, hair, and neckline of the dress. Taking the time to detail and highlight the portrait is what will bring the subject to life. This final stage in drawing portraits is what makes each subject unique from all other faces.

Now that we have completed the portrait, it is important to preserve the work, by applying a workable fixative to the final picture *(see manufacturer's directions for use)*. This will ensure that the final portrait does not smear or smudge and will maintain its completed look.

After completing the drawing, sit back and look at the different tonal values and the shifts of light that make up the beautiful characteristics of the portrait that you have just created. As John Ruskin has said, "Quality is never an accident. It is always the result of intelligent effort." The techniques and principles that have been shared in this text, and by taking the time to hone the skills of mastering an exact likeness, will give you confidence and quality in your work.

Congratulations!

You have made it to the end of this lesson!

Thank you for using this technical drawing technique. I am sure you will gain confidence and an understanding of drawing by using the Rite way!

You Can now draw with exact likeness!

"By the work one knows the workman."

~ Jean de La Fontaine

**You Can Draw Portraits:
Technical Drawing-Mastering an Exact Likeness** *(Drawing V)*

THE FINAL PORTRAIT

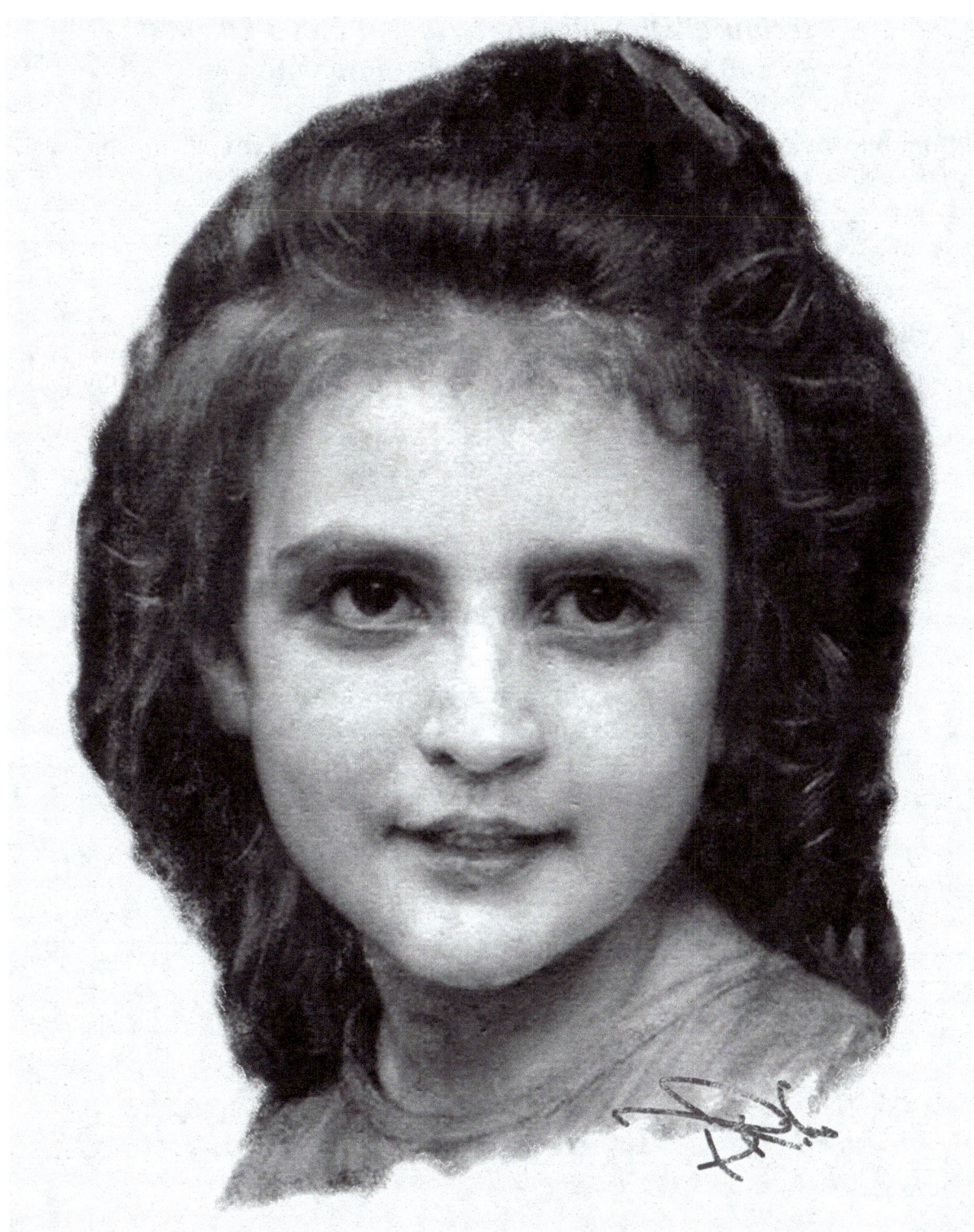

This has been an enjoyable experience for me to write this book for you. I hope that it has been informative, easy to understant, and has given you the confidence in your ability to draw. You can achieve the exact likeness of your subject when applying these exacting principles.

You Can Draw Portraits:
Technical Drawing-Mastering an Exact Likeness

I am thrilled that you have finished the lessons from
'Technical Drawing-Mastering an Exact Likeness'
and I would love to share more with you!

Look for my other instructional guides and books from my 'You Can' series
and add them to your collection today!

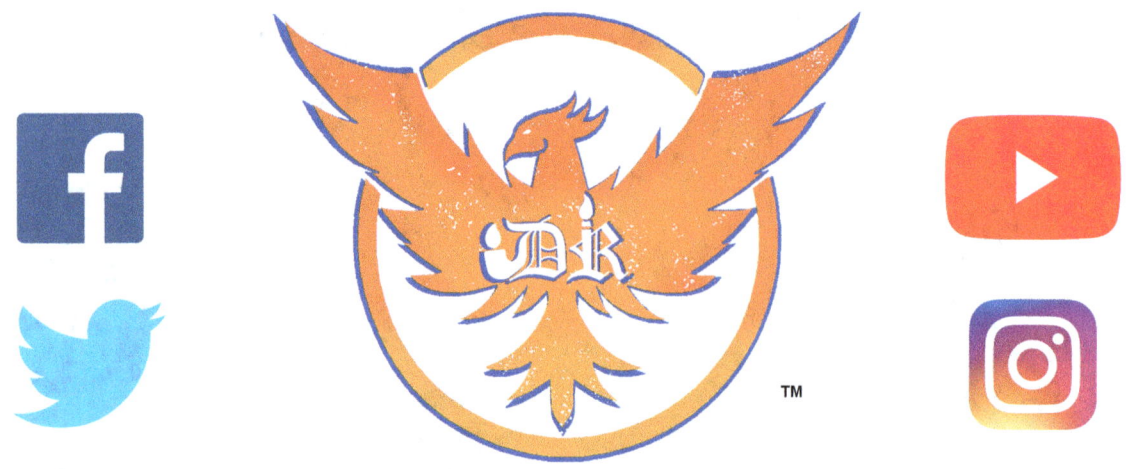

For more information and tutorials
visit my website at:

http://www.davidrite.com

Join our newsletter for exciting news, information, and sale promotions!
Be sure to tell your friends about us
and invite them to come and join the Rite program, too!

"Fortune favors the BOLD!"

~ Publius Terentius Afer
AKA Terence

APPENDIX:
Section: 8

"Art begins with resistance - at the point where resistance is overcome. No human masterpiece has ever been created without great labor"

~ Andre Gide

APPENDIX

APPENDIX

The fundamental reason for an artist to perfect their draftsmanship is to convey to the viewing audience the meaning of their work. The key to any good painting is the drawing underneath the paint. It is the substance or the essence of your pictorial work. The paint only serves as the harmonizing ingredient that makes the work more pleasing for the viewer. Be patient as it will take time to learn these exacting principles as you practice, practice, and practice; to make ready for the next phase, the paint.

The following pages are illustrations of the lines and angles that the artist uses for the placement of the subject on the canvas. The lines seen in this appendix are of the portrait that was used as the subject throughout this book. In addition to the face and hair, the lines for the subject's blouse, are included.

Each of the following illustrations should be viewed, from left to right, and top to bottom.

"We are what we repeatedly do. Excellence, then, is not an act, but a habit."

~ Aristotle

APPENDIX

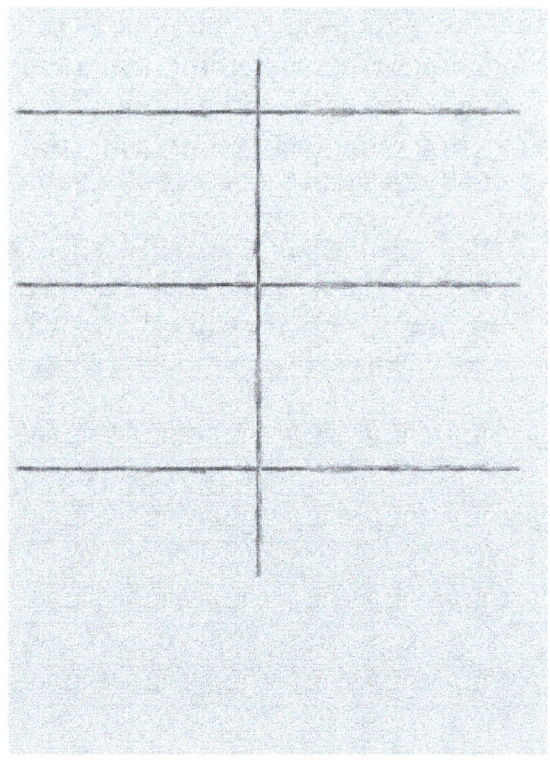
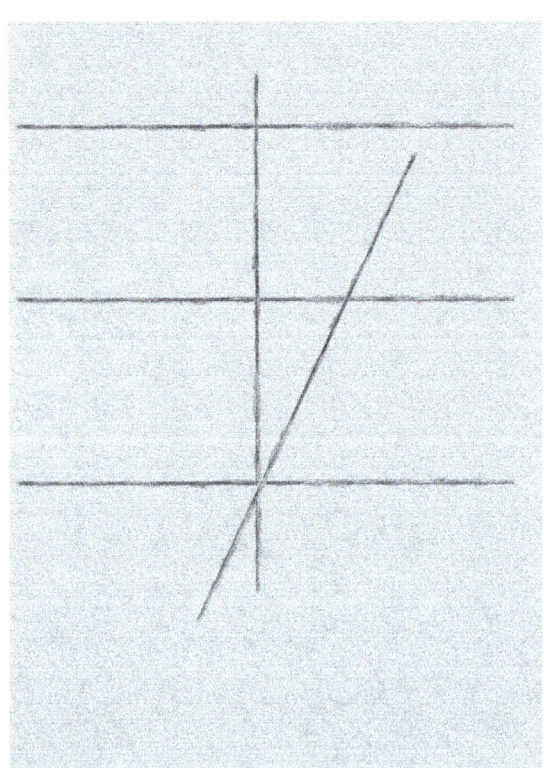
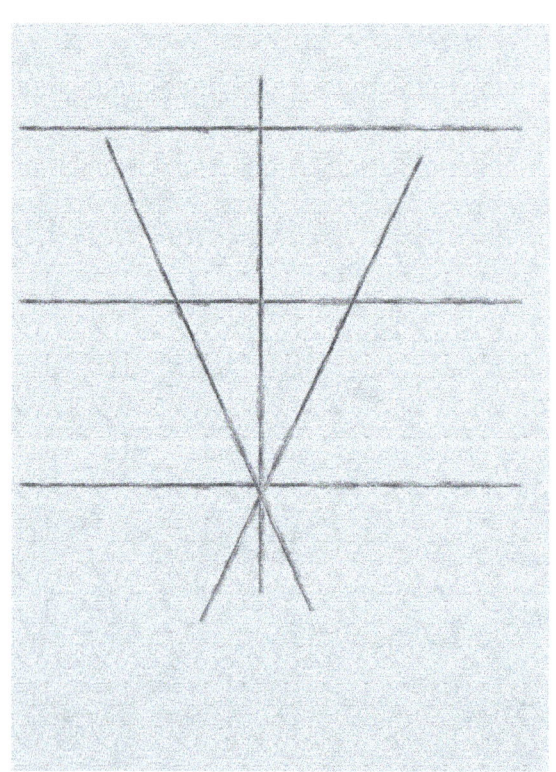

APPENDIX

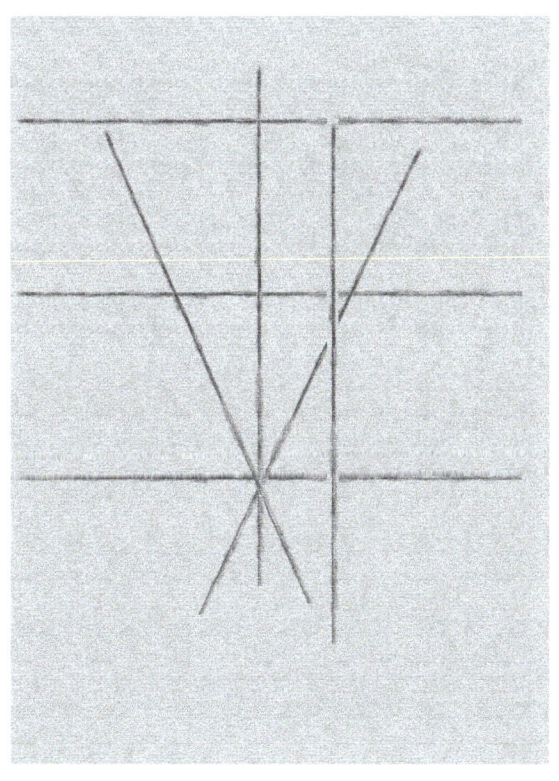
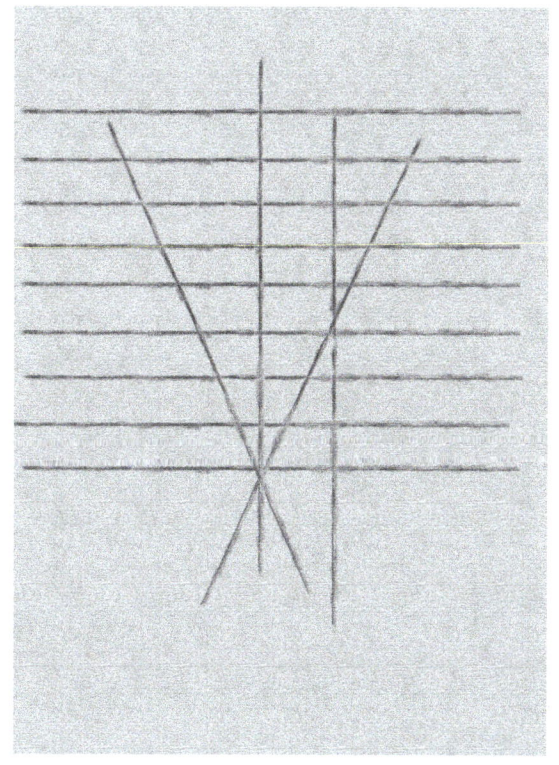
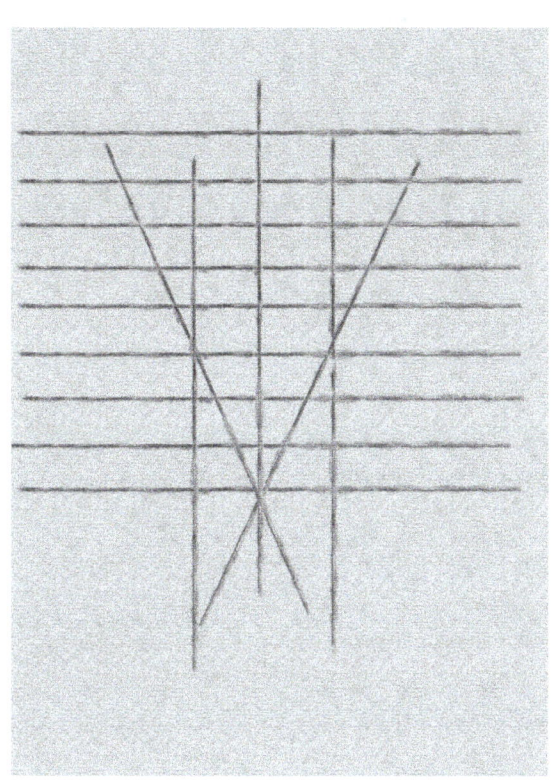
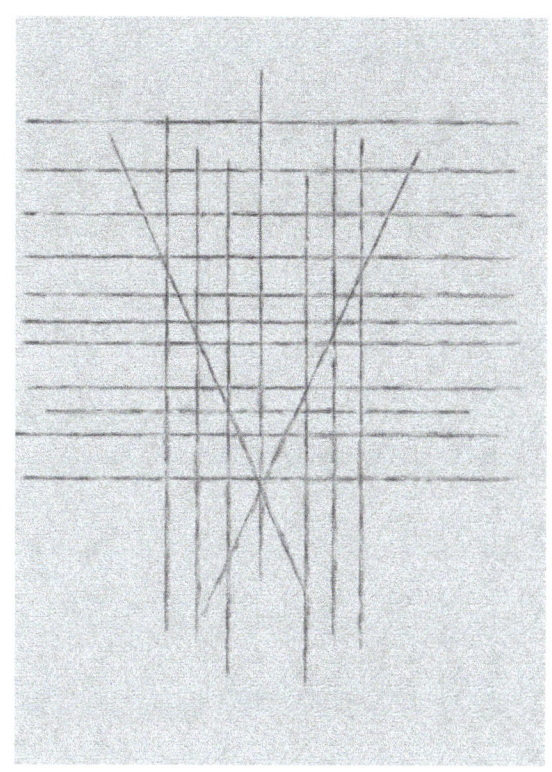

APPENDIX

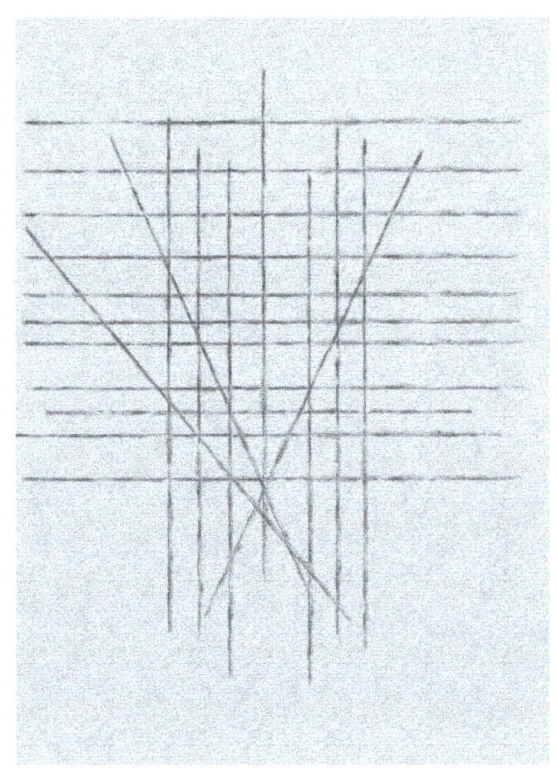
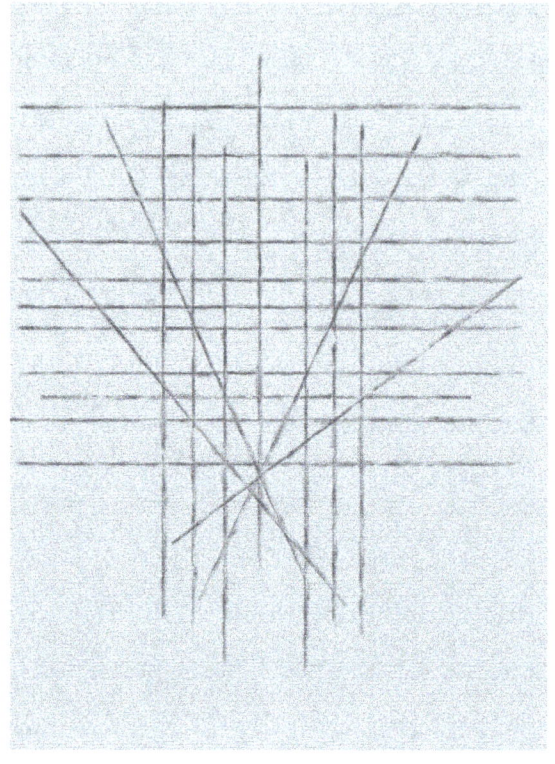
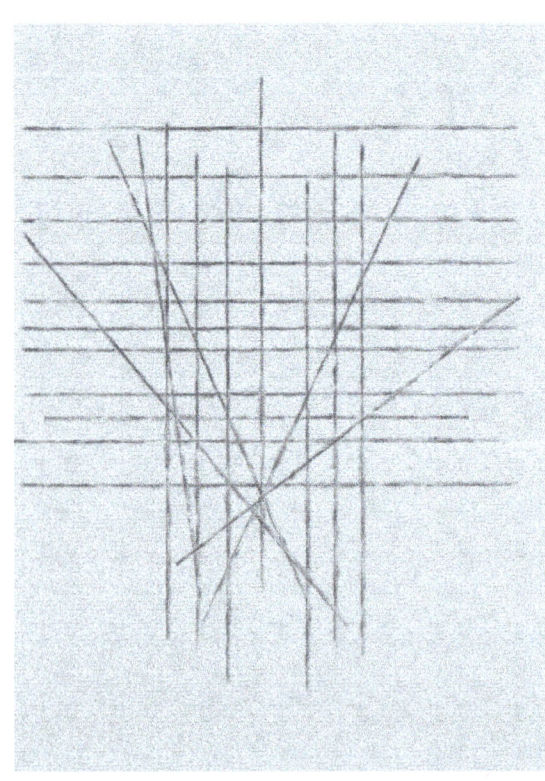
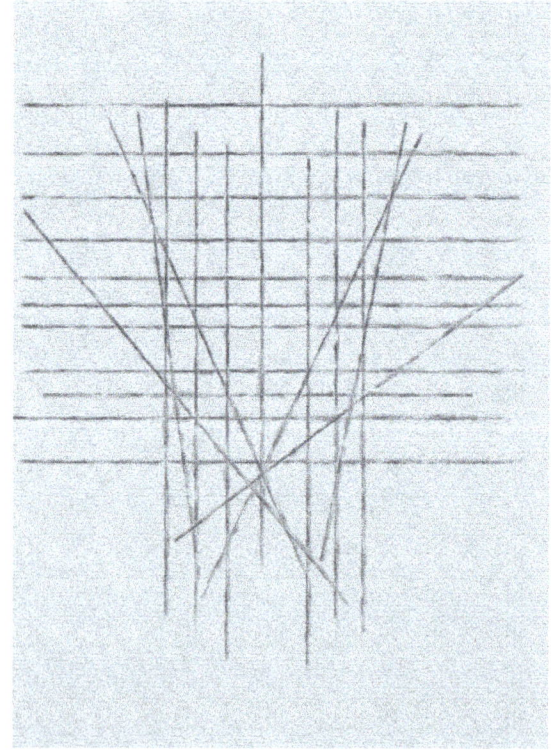

APPENDIX

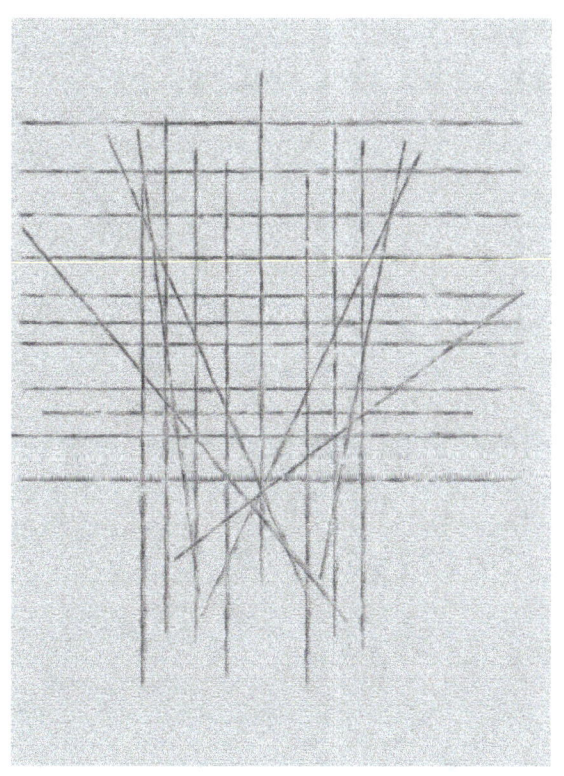
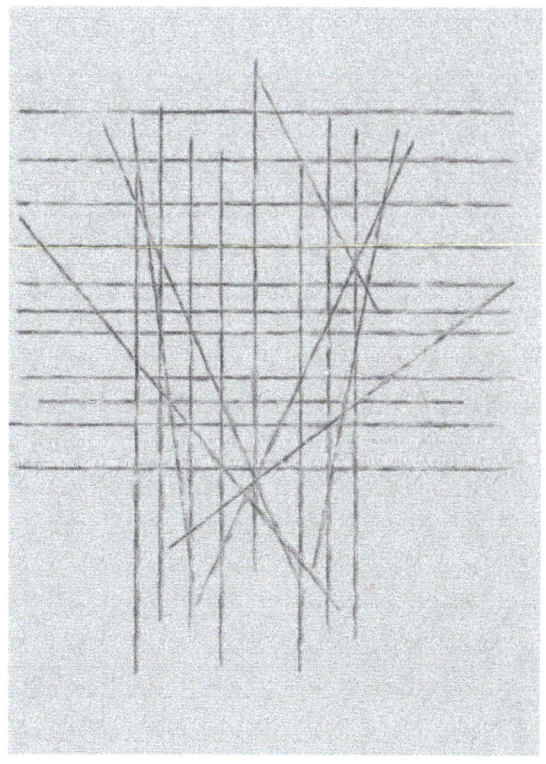
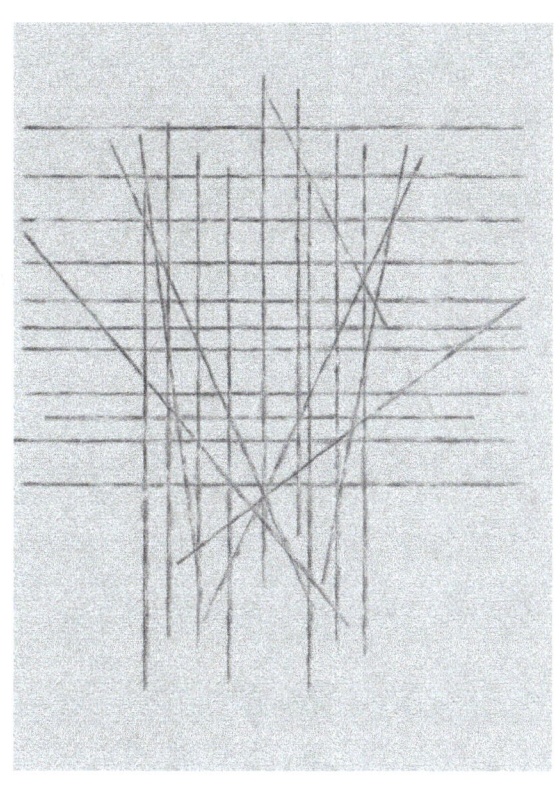
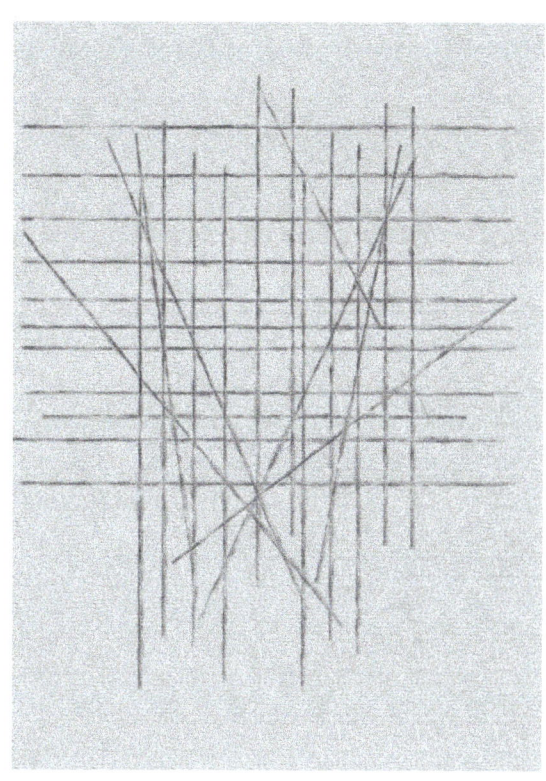

APPENDIX

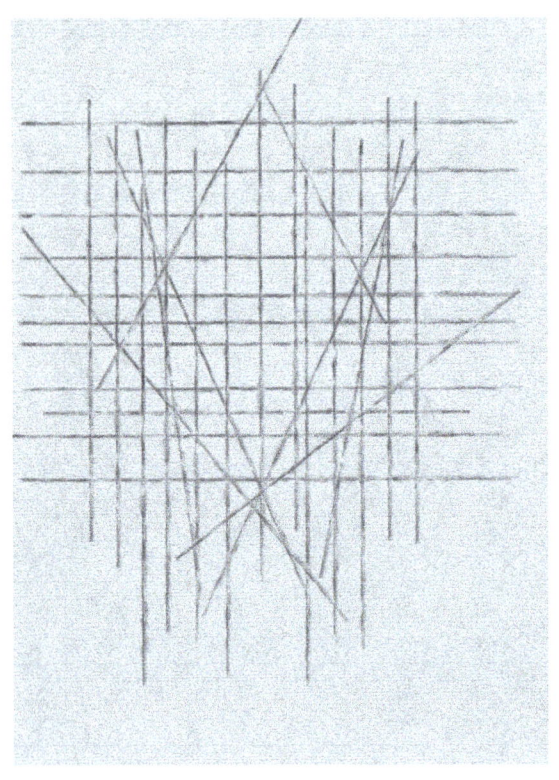
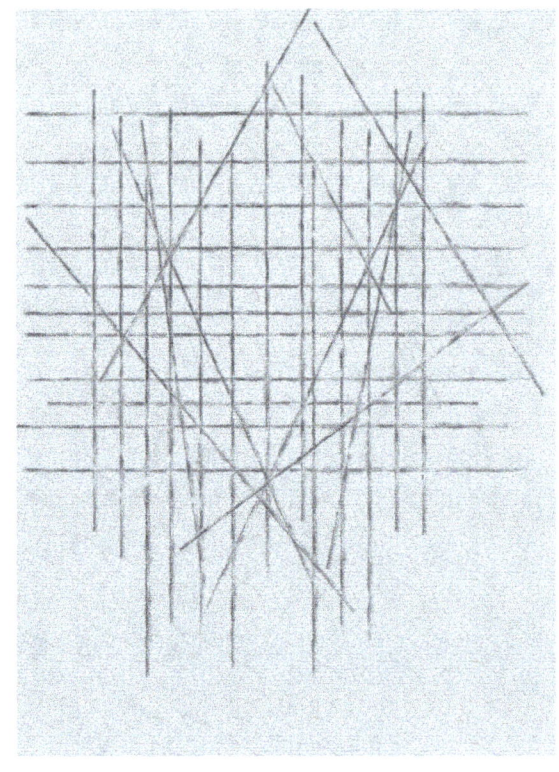
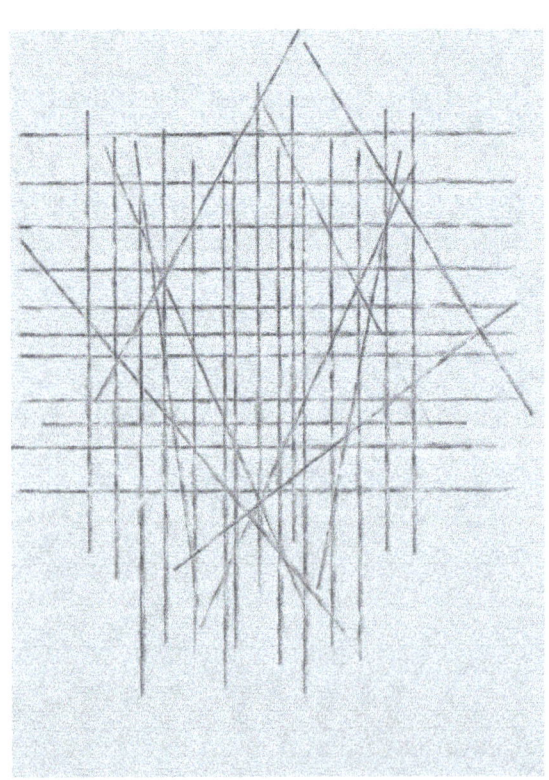
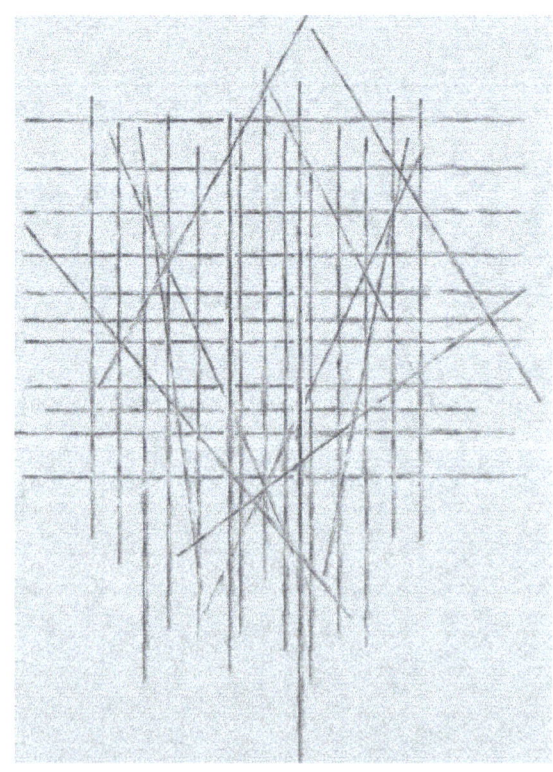

APPENDIX

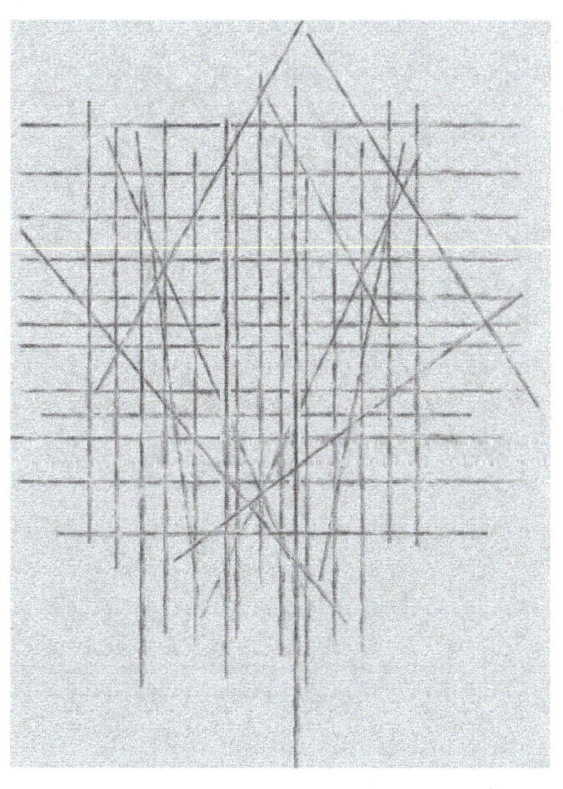
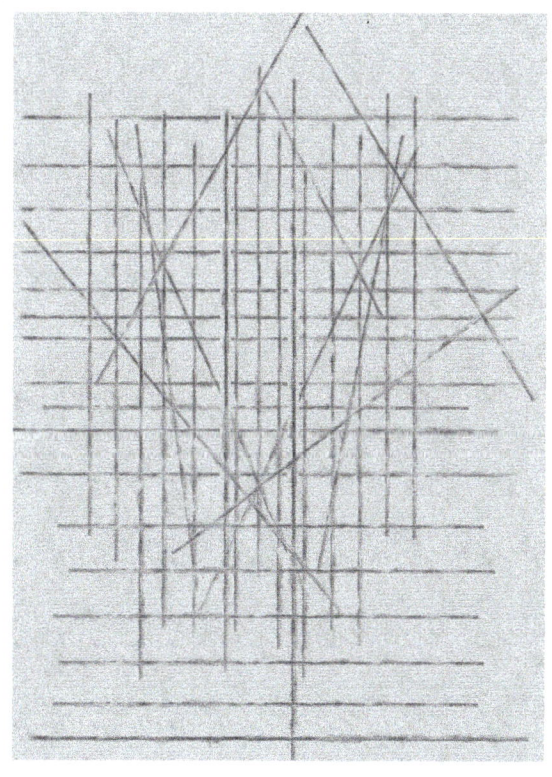
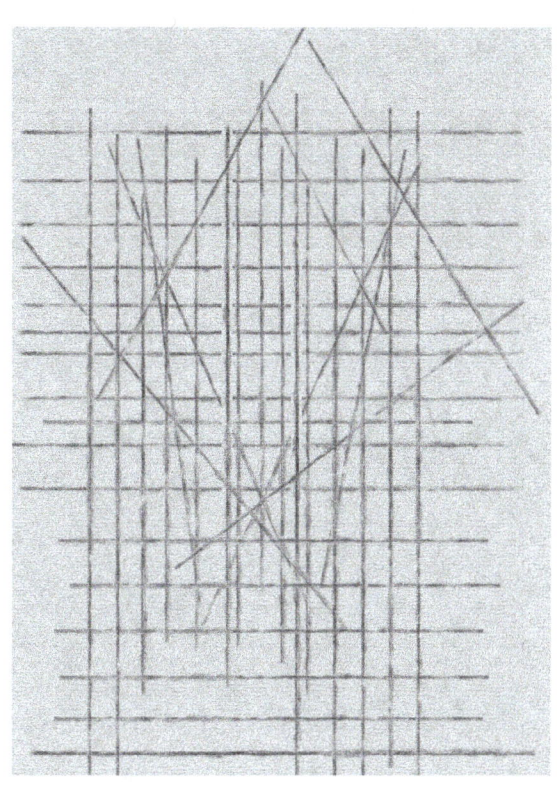
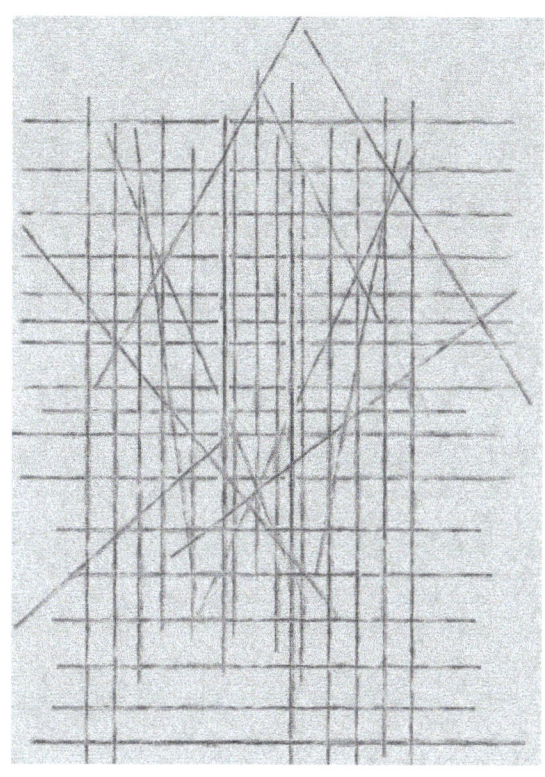

APPENDIX

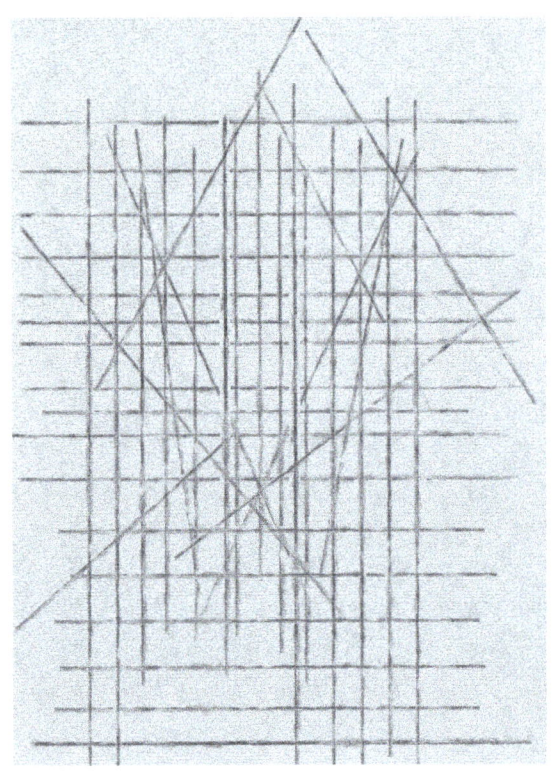
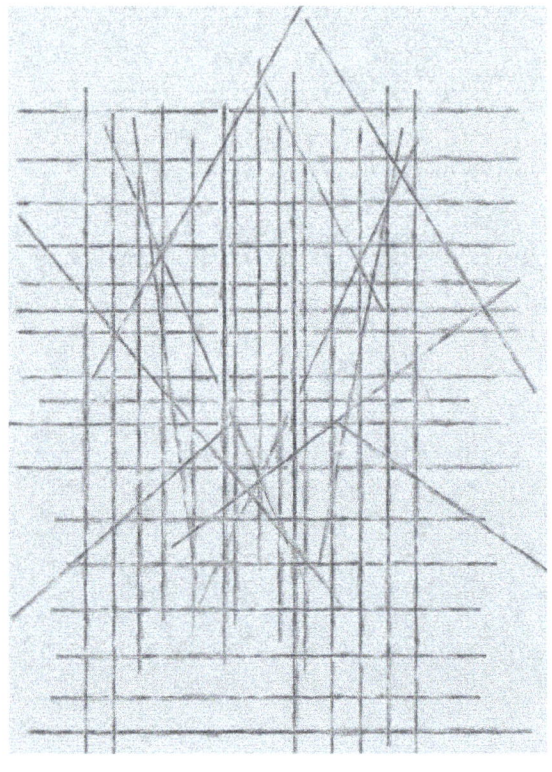
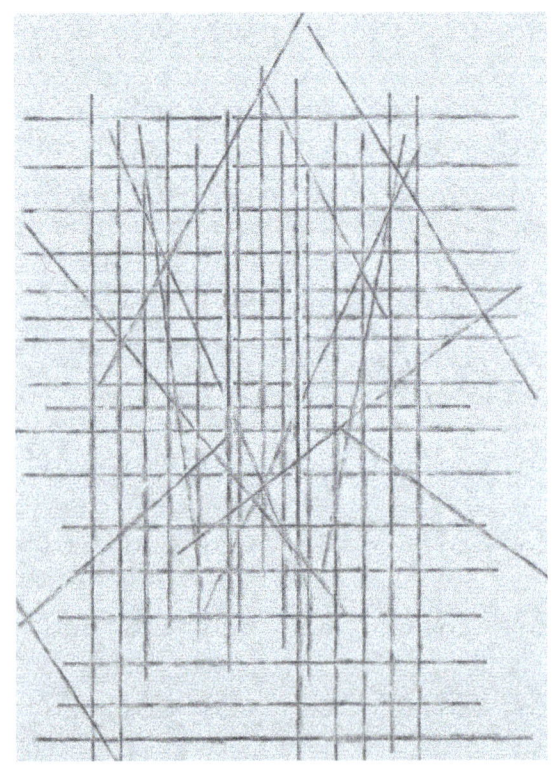
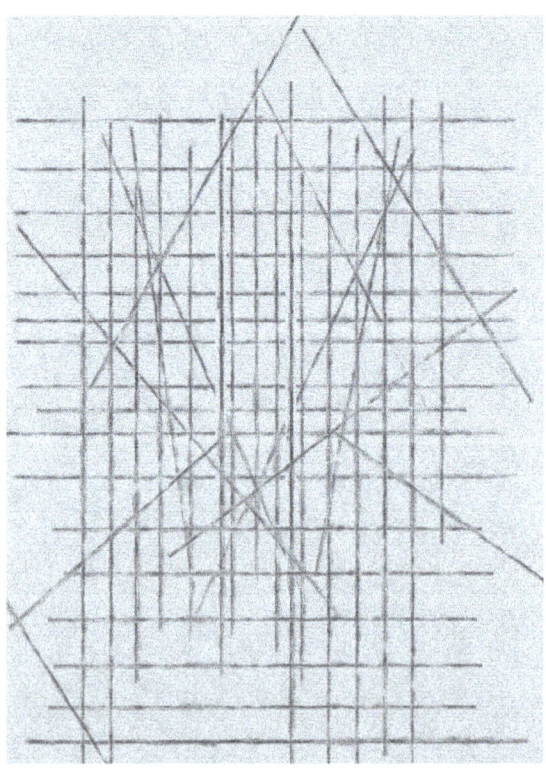

APPENDIX

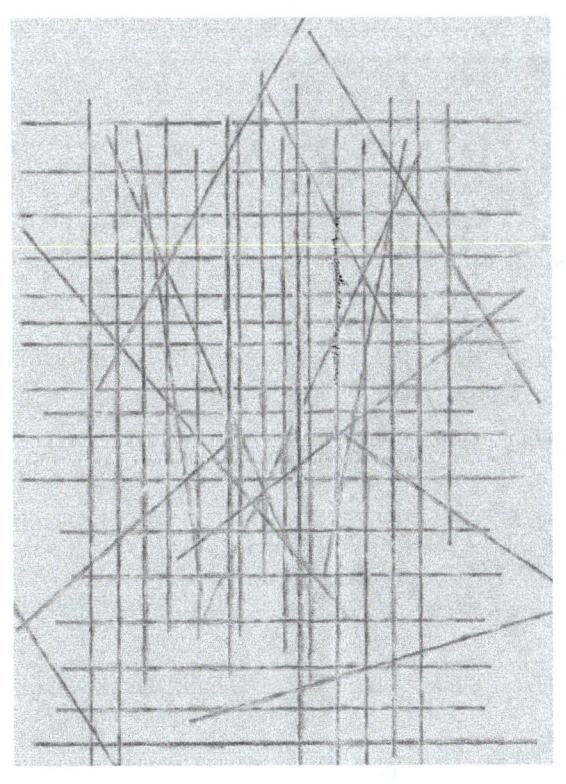

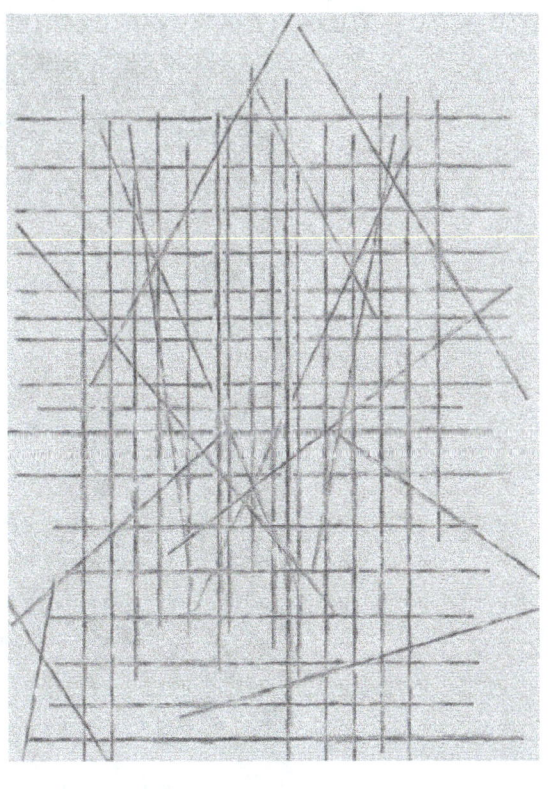

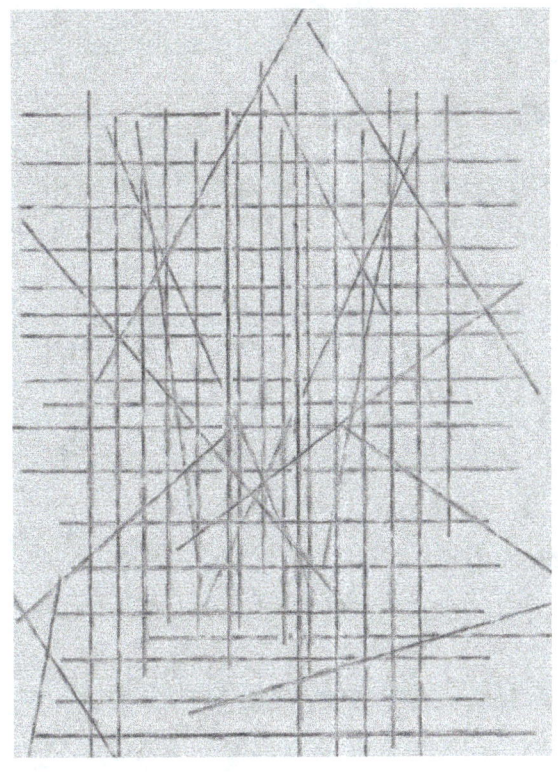

I have stated to my students;

"The key to a good painting is the drawing underneath the paint; it is the substance or the essence of your pictorial work. The paint only serves as the harmonizing ingredient that makes the work more pleasing for the viewer."

By using these systematic techniques shown in this book you too will have,

"a drawing as pleasing to the eye as a concerto is to the ears."

APPENDIX

In this section all the lines and angles have been illistrated to show
how to complete a portrait from start to finish!
It is that easy!
As these simple exacting and proven principles of drawing are followed then it becomes
almost effortless to accomplish beautiful drawings using this system.

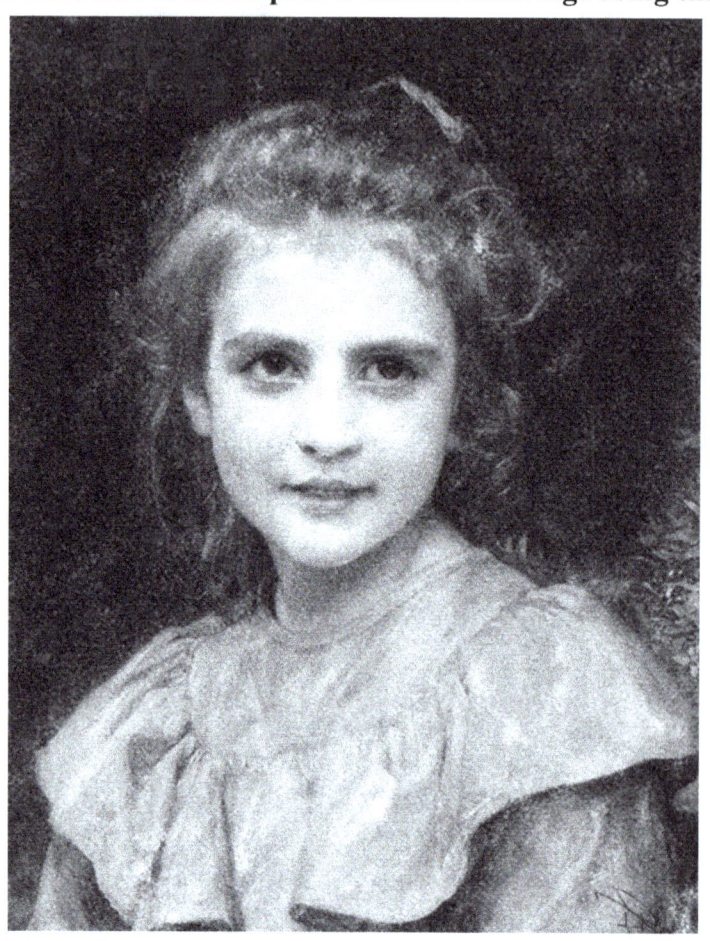

In this instructional book you have seen the systematic technique that has been used for repeated success by the classical and traditional masters of art.

It is a duplicatable and teachable system that can work for anyone who is willing to put forth the effort.

Using these techniques from this book, "You Can" bring a new perspective and life to your work. In return for your diligence and stick-to-itiveness, this may give you the opportunity you need to be confident in your work and could even make you a profit, too.

The best of luck to you!

GLOSSARY:
Section: 9

"Knowledge is power."

~ Sir Francis Bacon

GLOSSARY

ALPHABETICAL ORDER:

ANGLE(S): A measure of an angle or of the amount of turning necessary to bring one line or plane into coincidence with or parallel to another: The figure formed by two lines extending from the same point.

APEX: The highest part or point.

AXIS: An implied line in painting through a composition to which elements in the composition are referred: a line drawn and used as the basis of measurements in an architectural or other working drawing: a straight line with respect to which a body or figure is symmetrical: called also axis of symmetry: a straight line that bisects at right angles a system of parallel chords of a curve and divides the curve into two symmetrical parts.

BLEND: To combine or associate so that the line of demarcation cannot be distinguished.

CAST SHADOW: Is the imperfect and *(strong to faint)* representation of something cast upon a surface by a body intercepting the rays from a source of light. A cast shadow is a type of shadow that is created on a form next to a surface that is turned away from the source of light. When a form blocks the light, it causes a cast shadow to be formed. Every object that blocks light has a cast shadow associated with it.

COMPOSITION: Manner of being composed; structure: *"This painting has an orderly composition."*

CONCERTO: A piece for one or more soloists and orchestra with three contrasting movements.

CONCERTO GROSSO: Is a baroque orchestral composition featuring a small group of solo instruments contrasting with the full orchestra.

CONJUNCTION: The act or an instance of conjoining: the state of being conjoined or to join together.

CONTOURS: A line that traces the outer limits of an object or surface.

DARK TONE: Is the principal color of the work mixed with a darker color to make the color appear half darker than the principal color.

DETAIL: An individual or minute part; an item or particular.

DIAGONAL: An inclined obliquely from a reference line. A diagonal direction; a diagonal row, arrangement, or pattern; something oriented in diagonal position.

GLOSSARY

ALPHABETICAL ORDER:

EVENTUATE: To come out finally; to proceed or arise as a consequence, effect, or conclusion.

EYEBALL: Are organs that detect light and convert it to electro-chemical impulses in neurons. The simplest photoreceptors connect light to movement. In higher organisms' complex neural pathways exist that connect the eye, via the optic nerve to the visual cortex and other areas of the brain.

EYELID: Is a thin fold of skin that covers and protects the eye.

EYE SOCKET: The technical name for the eye socket is the orbit. The orbital bone is the cavity or socket of the skull in which the eye and its appendages are situated.

FORMULA: A conventionalized statement intended to express some fundamental truth or principle especially as a basis for negotiation or action.

FORESHORTENING: To shorten by proportionately contracting in the direction of depth so that an illusion of projection or extension in space is obtained.

GRAY SCALE: Images of the grayscale, also known as black and white, are composed exclusively of shades of gray, varying from black at the weakest intensity to white at the strongest. *SEE TONES FOR GRAY SCALE GRAPH*

HALFWAY POINT: Midway between two points or conditions: Reaching or including only half or a portion or partial.

HIGHLIGHT: The area of most intense light on a represented form, as in a painting or photograph.

HORIZON LINE: Also known as the HORIZONTAL LINE, in perspective drawing the 'horizon line', is a line strait across the picture. Horizon line is the 'imaginary line' drawn by the artist. The horizon line is at your eye level, the position where you are looking from, whether from above or below and is decided by where the horizontal line is placed on your canvas.

HUES: Is one of the main properties of a color, defined technically as "the degree to which a stimulus can be described as similar to or different from stimuli that are described as red, green, blue, and yellow. In painting color theory, a hue refers to a pure color, one without tint or shade *(added white or black pigment, respectively)*. A hue is an element of the color wheel.

GLOSSARY

ALPHABETICAL ORDER:

ILLUSTRATED: To make clear by giving or by serving as an example or instance: to provide with visual features intended to explain or decorate.

INSTRUMENT: A means whereby something is achieved, performed, or furthered: one used by another as a means or aids, i.e. a tool.

INTERRELATED: Having a mutual or reciprocal relation *(to bring into mutual relation)*.

IRIS: The iris is a diaphragm of variable size whose function is to adjust the size of the pupil to regulate the amount of light admitted into the eye. The iris is the colored part of the eye.

JUNCTION: A place where two or more things are united or the act or an instance of joining two or more things into one.

MAIN LIGHT (DIRECT): Is also known, as the key light, is the first and usually most important main light that illuminates a subject. The purpose of the key light is to highlight the form and dimension of a subject. The key light is not a rigid requirement; omitting the key light can result in a silhouette effect.

MAIN LIGHT (SOURCE): It is the direction of light, or where the main or whole of light is facing; in the case of 'The Main Light Source' it is the most light being shown on an object.

MATERIAL: The basic elements from which something can be developed, or the items needed for the performance of a task or activity.

MEASURE / MEASUREMENTS / LIMIT LINE(S): The dimensions, capacity, or amount of something ascertained by measuring: an estimate of what is to be expected: a measured quantity or the act or process of measuring. Visual representations of the specified limits for a measurement.

MEDIOCRE: Of moderate or low quality, value, ability, or performance. Moderate to inferior in quality: ordinary or so-so.

MONOCHROME: The state or condition of being painted, decorated, etc., in shades of a single color.

ONE-TWO POINT PERSPECTIVE: A mathematical system for representing three-dimensional objects and space on a two-dimensional surface by means of intersecting lines that are drawn vertically and horizontally and that radiate from one point *(one-point perspective)*, two points *(two-point perspective)*, or several points on a horizon line as perceived by a viewer imagined in an arbitrarily fixed position.

GLOSSARY

ALPHABETICAL ORDER:

OUTLINE: The line by which a figure or object is defined or bounded; contour.

PERSPECTIVE: A technique of depicting volumes and spatial relationships on a flat surface.

PROCESS: To subject to a special process or treatment: to subject to or handle through an established usually routine set of procedures.

PUPIL: The pupil is the aperture through which light - and hence the images we *"see"* and *"perceive"* - enters the eye that is formed by the iris. As the size of the iris increases *(or decreases)* the size of the pupil decreases *(or increases)* correspondingly.

REFERENCE POINT: Are also MAP POINTS. A point to which other points, lines, and so forth are referred, usually in terms of distance or direction, or both.

REFLECTED LIGHT: Can be seen by the light they emit, or, more often, by the light they reflect. Reflected light obeys the law of reflection, that the angle of reflection equals the angle of incidence.

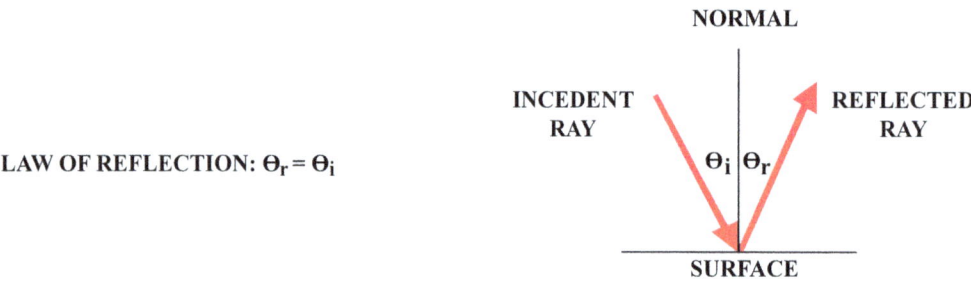

LAW OF REFLECTION: $\theta_r = \theta_i$

RESTATE: To express something *(as a text, statement or subject)* in different words.

SHADOW: A dark figure or image cast on some surface by a body intercepting light. A shadow is an area where direct light from a light source cannot reach due to obstruction by an object. It occupies all of the space behind an opaque object with light in front of it. The cross section of a shadow is a two-dimensional silhouette, or reverse projection of the object blocking the light. Also known as DEEP SHADOWS which is the darkness caused by something preventing light from reaching a place or to cover something with a dark or deep shadow.

SLOPE: Something that slants; sloping - often used in combination *(slope-sided)*.

STAGE(S): A period or step in a process, activity, or development: as one of the distinguishable periods of growth and development of a talent or art piece. A period or phase in a course of direction or the degree of involvement or one passing through a *(specified)* stage.

GLOSSARY

ALPHABETICAL ORDER:

TONE(S): A phenomenon of light or visual perception that enables one to differentiate otherwise identical objects. There are also TONAL VALUES, which in art, tone refers to the degree of lightness or darkness of an area. Tone varies from the bright white of a light source through shades of gray to the deepest black shadows. *(See the grayscale below)*

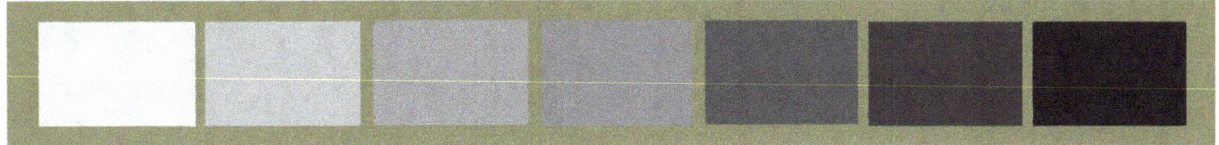

TRANSFER / TRANSFERRED: To print or otherwise copy from one surface to another by contact.

VALUE(S): A quality that gives something special worth or the relative usefulness or importance of something as judged by specific qualities. In art, *value* is often referring to the relation to color theory. Value in art is essentially how light or dark something is on a scale of white to black *(or the grayscale)*. White being the *highest value* and black being the *lowest value*.

VANISHING POINT: A point of disappearance *(in the study of perspective in art)* that point toward which receding parallel lines appear to converge.

VARIATION: The act or process of varying: a different or distinct form or version of something.

VERTICAL LINE: In perspective drawing the *'Vertical Line'* is a line strait across the picture or canvas in a north to south *(or visa-versa)* direction. Vertical line is the 'imaginary line' or literal line drawn by the artist.

VIRTUOSO: One skilled in or having a taste for the fine art: a person who has great skill at some endeavor.

"Education is not the filling of a pail, but the lighting of a fire."

~ William Butler Yeats

MATERIALS DEFINED

ALPHABETICAL ORDER:

CHARCOAL PAPER (TEXTURED):

This will allow the detail needed to polish your work. There are many types of paper used in drawing with charcoal, so choose one that will give the most advantage in drawing. Generally that will be the one that allows for fine detail.

CHARCOAL STICK (FINE VINE):

These fine vine charcoal pieces are for obtaining the intricate detail in the finished work.

CHARCOAL STICK (NUMBER 9):

This is one of the most important beginning tools as it keeps the drawing simple and adds essential working material for finding the tonal values. Number 9 is what I used, however it can be hard to find. A 16mm stick may be used to acheive the desired look.

CHARCOAL STUMPS:

Several sizes will be needed. These stumps are used as blending tools that can obtain important tonal values.

KNEADED ERASERS:

The kneaded eraser is a subtracting tool that can be used to draw with. After placing charcoal onto the paper it can highlight, erase, or draw subtal tonal shifts with this important tool.

MEASURING TOOL:

Some kind of measuring tool will be needed. Use a pencil, brush, ruler ect. I use a mechanical drawing pencil.

TORILLONS:

Several sizes will be needed. These are used instead of your fingers for blending and smoothing.

WHITE COMPRESSED CHARCOAL:

Usesd for correcting mistakes and toning.

MATERIALS DEFINED

ALPHABETICAL ORDER:

WORKABLE FIXATIVE:

To save your work from accidental smearing.

I am thrilled that you have finished this instructional book.
There is more to share with you!

Look for my other instructional guides and books from my 'You Can' series
and add them to your collection today!

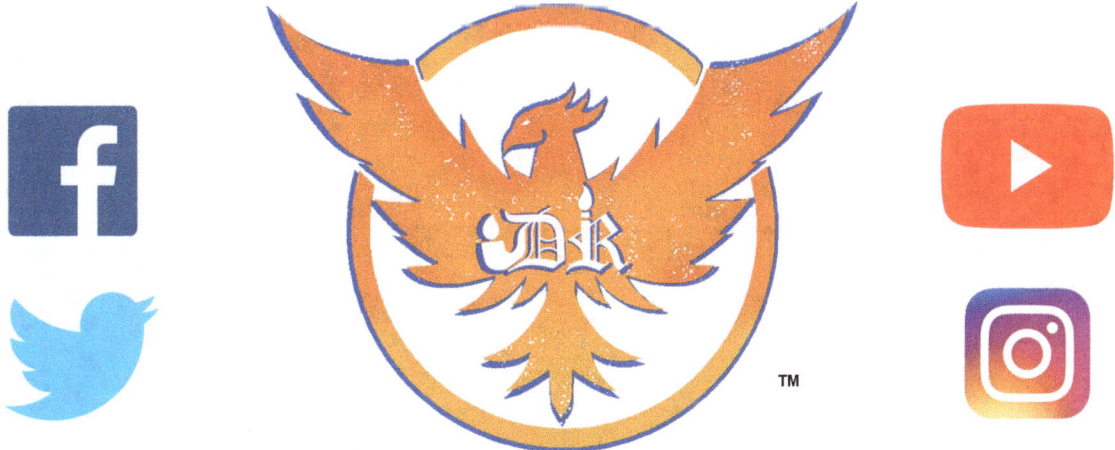

For more information and tutorials
visit my website at:

http://www.davidrite.com

*Join our newsletter for exciting news, information, and sale promotions!
Be sure to tell your friends about us
and invite them to come and join the Rite program, too!*

"In order to get the best results, you need to use the RITE tool, for the RITE job."

~ David Rite

www.ingramcontent.com/pod-product-compliance
Lightning Source LLC
Chambersburg PA
CBHW062324220526
45469CB00008B/2612